# *In This Moment Daily Meditation Book*

**SECOND EDITION**

*In This Moment Daily Meditation Book*
is CoDA Conference endorsed literature.
Copyright date here

Second Edition
First Printed 2006
Reprinted 2011, 2020
Codependents Anonymous, Inc
All rights reserved.
This publication may not be reproduced
or photocopied without written permission of
Codependents Anonymous, Inc

To obtain additional copies of *In This Moment Daily Meditations*,
and all other CoDA Conference endorsed literature, contact
CoDA Resource Publishing, Inc:

**CoRe Publications**
www.corepublications.org
1-805-297-8114
info@corepublications.org

For general information about CoDA, contact:

**Co-Dependents Anonymous, Inc**
For general information about CoDA
www.coda.org
info@coda.org
PO Box 33577
Phoenix, AZ 85067-3577, USA
1-602-227-7991
Toll free: 1-888-444-2359
Spanish Toll Free: 1-888-444-2379

*ISBN-13: 978-0-9647105-1-1*

*For the Fellowship*

# JANUARY 1

## *In This Moment, I welcome the New Year.*

This is a day when I think about the past year and make resolutions for the coming year. TV programs and newspapers cover the themes "the best of" and "the worst of" in the old year. I like to contemplate last year's growth and to give thought to possible improvements in my behavior in the year to come.

If I just do the best I can in this moment, as each moment follows another, they add up to a good day. One day at a time, with my Higher Power's help, each of these days well lived adds up to a lifetime of abundant living.

# JANUARY 2

## *In This Moment,*
## *I know this pain will end.*

I know there will be more occasions of pain in my life. I know there will be more occasions of happiness and joy.

Becoming an observer of my life helps me to see there will be both joy and pain. Recovery teaches me to work through the pain and to revel in the happiness. There WILL be both.

I learn from the pain and know I will be happy again.

# JANUARY 3

## *In This Moment, I feel whole.*

Often, I feel weary and depressed, dragging myself through daily life. I feel "less than," sad, and codependent.

Not today! Attending a CoDA event this past weekend energized my recovery. Talking with people who value and practice CoDA principles is an opportunity I cherish. Right now I feel whole, emotionally and spiritually. My soul is filled with gratitude for CoDA friends and a Higher Powered experience.

# JANUARY 4

## *In This Moment, I study my motivation.*

Higher Power, please help me to be aware of my motives. When I perform acts of kindness, I need to know why I perform them. Am I being codependent? Am I motivated from the desire to gain the approval of others? If I am, please help me to change.

I seek to grow into a person who performs acts of kindness for healthy reasons.

# JANUARY 5

## *In This Moment, I ask for God's help.*

Oftentimes, before I try to do something different, fear waits for me at the door, keeping me from experimenting with new behaviors. As a result, I continue to do what's comfortable instead of what's healthy. I need to do three things to change this pattern: ask God for help, believe God is helping me, and take action.

Asking for help requires some effort, because it's hard to commit to change. After I ask for God's help, the next step involves the practical application of my faith. Even if I can't convince myself that God is helping me right now, I can "act as if" God is helping me through this stage of recovery. I take positive action. I can accomplish what used to baffle and paralyze me. I act with new confidence and commitment to purpose. Then hope and integrity return to my life.

# JANUARY 6

## *In This Moment, I remember Max.*

I often tell people my best relationship was with my dog. He and I had a wonderful, loving, and intimate relationship. I loved to put my face on his warm, hairy coat. I loved his enthusiastic greeting when I came home.

He accepted me exactly as I am. More amazingly, I accepted Max exactly as he was. Being codependent, I have trouble accepting people as they are. I still want to change my husband — even after five years in CoDA.

At all times, Max knew how he felt. He lived in the moment, fully and completely. He was a role model for me. He was a puppy when he came to live with us and Max died at age fifteen. I miss him.

# JANUARY 7

## *In This Moment, I do not have to do anything.*

When I am faced with a painful reality, when I don't like the plan, I reach into my heart and remember my Higher Power's plan is greater than any I could imagine. I ask for help in coming to acceptance. I look to Steps One, Two, and Three, and realize I am powerless. I have made a decision to believe in a Higher Power and I have decided to turn my will and my life over to this Higher Power. In so doing, I am relieved of the pressure to do something. I live in the moment and accept what is.

# JANUARY 8

## *In This Moment, what about me?*

Before CoDA, I was selfish, insecure, and took everything personally. It was always, "Why are they doing this to me?" "Why does this happen to me?" "What is wrong with me?" It was a selfish "me."

In recovery, I'm learning what healthy relationships are and, more importantly, how to be in them. What give and take means. Accepting others exactly as they are, even though their thoughts, ideas, and actions are different than mine. I have choices of participating in relationships or accepting that certain relationships are not good for me.

# JANUARY 9

# *In This Moment,*
# *I keep my prayers simple.*

Before I go inside to work, I meditate for five minutes in my truck. It always calms me down and helps me get centered. I like to keep it simple. I say, "God, please help me to see your will for me today and give me the power to carry that out." And it works! At night, I say some form of thank you prayer, sometimes even for the difficulties I've endured that day.

Sometimes, I forget to pray and meditate. When this happens, I try not to be too hard on myself. I return to my prayer and meditation as soon as I can.

My Higher Power is always there to welcome me back.

# JANUARY 10

## *In This Moment, I'm not in control.*

Admit complete defeat? Not me! When I came into CoDA, I was my own Higher Power. I was doing just fine on my own, thank you! The God I knew then was not kind or loving, so why would I admit anything to God?

Now, I totally accept Step One. When I came to believe that a loving Higher Power is in charge, I became able to let go of my need to control outcomes. I stepped down from the director's chair and let the world run as it's supposed to: under my Higher Power's direction.

# JANUARY 11

# *In This Moment,*
# *I appreciate my own company.*

I'm so powerless over the weather! It's a chilly winter's day in New England. Blowing wind and snow. I bundled myself up in gloves, hat, two layers of fleece, and took myself out to lunch. I sipped some cocoa, read a newspaper, and took my time. I didn't feel lonely. I was enjoying myself, by myself. How great is that? One of the joys of recovery is learning to love the self. I don't always love myself or like myself. I can feel ashamed and be self-critical. But today I let go of all that. I enjoyed my own company. It says in CoDA's *Welcome* that God intends us to be "precious and free." Today, I feel it.

# JANUARY 12

# *In This Moment,*
# *I am getting off the pity pot.*

Early in my recovery, I resented that phrase "get off the pity pot." I clung fiercely to my self-pity. It was mine, I earned it, and it was nobody else's business. In some vague way, I realized it was about the only shred of self that I had left. As time passed and I worked my program, I began to recover more of my authentic self. I had less need for my self-pity and I came to see how destructive it is. In my codependency, I needed self-pity to survive, but in my recovery, self-pity only keeps me stuck in my misery.

In this moment, I let go of self-pity. Using the Steps and Traditions leads me to faith, acceptance, and serenity.

# JANUARY 13

# *In This Moment,*
# *I'm asking God.*

I've been thinking about how often I complain to my Higher Power, whom I choose to call God. I say things like, "I'm grateful for this, God, but…" or, "I know I'm powerless, but…" Then the thought came to me: Don't tell God what to do! I describe the problem, turn it over, and then ask what I need to do.

When I do this with faith, God shows me what, if anything, I need to do. I trust that God's answer is better than any I could come up with myself.

# JANUARY 14

## *In This Moment,*
## *I have a new voice.*

In recovery, I discovered my favorite feeling: Joy. Feelings overwhelmed me before CoDA. For a while, I didn't know that I had feelings.

Now, I smile with awareness and rejoice in gratitude. I wrestle with fear, anger, and hurt. A new spirit drives me. I don't doubt my authenticity; there is a new voice I call my own. I feel a new power within.

# JANUARY 15

## *In This Moment,*
## *I am true to myself.*

"To thine own self be true" is on all my CoDA chips. This is what "authentic" means to me. I used to be such a people-pleaser. I lost my identity and myself. I didn't know what I wanted or that it mattered. It was more important to make other people happy, anticipating their needs and wants, despite the cost to myself. I was proud that I could do that for my husband, family, friends, and co-workers.

Today, I am proud that my happiness comes first. I know who I am and what I like. I am assertive about asking for what I want or need. My life changed because I changed myself.

# JANUARY 16

## *In This Moment, I am real.*

In my group's meeting room there is a glass-encased collection of beautiful and unusual dolls. As a codependent, I was like one of those dolls. I tried to be perfect and bent myself into any shape just to be picked. I dressed up, sat on a shelf, and waited for someone to start my life. If only I were pretty enough and patient enough, someone would pick me. My life would be the "happily ever after" of fairy tales.

In recovery, I live life my way; I choose myself. I don't wait for a friend, a job, or a mate to start my life. I am a person with unique gifts, talents, and characteristics for which I am grateful. I have all I need. I am not a doll. I am real.

# JANUARY 17

## *In This Moment, I am able to listen.*

I wonder why "listening" isn't taught in school. No one taught me how to listen; many times I felt nobody listened to me. I didn't know how to listen to others or even to myself.

Since I've been attending CoDA meetings regularly, I'm learning to listen to others — really listen, instead of worrying what they're thinking about me. I hear the words and the feelings behind those words. I pay attention to what it feels like to be heard. When I am heard, I feel validated and I'm more open to hearing others. It's a wonderful circle.

# JANUARY 18

## *In This Moment, I move into my strength and power.*

The icy fear that paralyzed me is beginning to melt. Deep inside me resides a fiery strength and power. It lay dormant for years. Now, in recovery, it calls to me. I stand on my own two feet. With these feet I walk through the Twelve Steps. Sometimes the responsibility scares me, but it is also empowering. If I fall, I can get back up. I have choices. I make my own decisions. I am strong.

# JANUARY 19

## *In This Moment, I let go and let God.*

When I surrender, I allow my Higher Power to do for me what I cannot do for myself. This releases me from the stress to perform and fear of failure. When I stop, drop, and pray, I give myself time to refocus. I especially like the *Serenity Prayer* because it is simple, direct, and powerful. It helps me realign my priorities. The benefits are inner peace that money can't buy, the courage to be all that I can be, and the wisdom to know I'm not in control.

I see a miraculous change in my life. Today, I am in the flow of my Higher Power's will for my life.

# JANUARY 20

## *In This Moment,*
## *I hear my Higher Power.*

What does my Higher Power want for me? How do I learn that? I hear the voice of my Higher Power in many ways. It's a mystery how it works. I connect to my Higher Power by going to meetings, making my calls, talking to other CoDA members, being still, resting, or talking to my sponsor. I discern my Higher Power's guidance during regular times of prayer and meditation. Each day, as I practice Step Eleven, I ask my Higher Power to show me what to do today and help me do it.

I trust that my Higher Power's plan for me is one of fullness, abundance, and joy. "Thank you, God," is all I need to say.

# **JANUARY 21**

## *In This Moment, I am grateful.*

I have a sound roof over my head.
I have a comfortable bed in which to sleep.
I eat well and my dog loves me.
I have enough money to pay my bills.
I can walk, talk, hear, and see.
For all this and more, I am grateful.

# JANUARY 22

## *In This Moment, I have a loving guide.*

There are countless positive paths within the Steps. The one I cherish is the Third Step, which gives me the freedom to choose a God of my understanding. For the first time in my life, I feel free to choose. My codependence kept me stuck and fearful of making choices. Steps One and Two give me the gift of hope that there is a way out of my misery and the courage to accept the freedom offered in the Third Step. Now, I know that my freely chosen Higher Power guides me lovingly in every life choice.

# JANUARY 23

## *In This Moment, my heart is open.*

The deep despair of this deafening quiet opens my heart to ask God, "Speak to me, please. What is it you want? Why is it so hard? What would you have me do in this moment right now?"

I feel lost. My relationship is troubled. Am I the aggressor? If so, I ask to have that character defect removed.

I work my program. I speak with an open heart. I ask with an open mind. I turn to my Higher Power. I seek guidance. I breathe. In the quiet, my Higher Power answers.

# JANUARY 24

## *In This Moment, I am frustrated.*

People and events are not moving along fast enough for me. Recovery teaches me to ask myself, "How much control do I have over any of this?" Today, the answer is, "None." The solution? Silently, I recite the *Serenity Prayer*. I thank my Higher Power for the wisdom of recovery thinking. There will always be difficult situations. I'm learning to handle them differently. My frustration fades as I let go and let God.

# JANUARY 25

## *In This Moment,*
## *I am more than the sum of my mistakes and misfortunes.*

I accept my codependent tendencies while honoring my value and worth. All the experiences that led to my recovery are gifts, too. My recovery provides me with new insights and grants me wisdom that makes me a happier person. I may choose to share this knowledge with others, inside or outside the CoDA Fellowship. My recovery is a gift from my Higher Power, without which I would not be the person I am today.

# JANUARY 26

## *In This Moment, I am gentle with myself.*

I forgive myself for my past mistakes and focus on the lessons I've learned. I have compassion for myself, for all the trials and pain that I have endured. I acknowledge my accomplishments instead of always thinking how much more I have to do. I allow myself to observe and notice without judging or reacting. Each small step, each daily action, is what counts in recovery.

# JANUARY 27

# *In This Moment,*
# *I accept my relationships.*

It took me years to admit to being codependent. I blamed others when relationships failed. I was OK; they were selfish. I expected them to be perfect. If they had defects, I thought I could change them.

In CoDA, I've learned that I can only change myself. I accept that no one is perfect. Today, I love and accept others. I work on being honest in my relationships. Promise Seven is possible: "I am capable of developing and maintaining healthy relationships."

# JANUARY 28

# *In This Moment, I fit in.*

One of my challenges in life and recovery is to stop replaying my childhood drama. I have an older sister, and I was also the youngest in my extended family of aunts, uncles, and cousins. My relatives lived within a block of us and we socialized daily. But there was no space for me. I felt "apart from" and "less than." I had no voice.

In CoDA, I feel heard. I experience a sense of community within the Fellowship. I feel connected to other members. Here — I fit in.

# JANUARY 29

## *In This Moment, I'm pleased with my decision.*

One way that my codependence manifests itself is by avoiding decisions. I worry and postpone, uncertain if I'm making the best possible choice — even though I know in my head there's no one perfect choice.

I've been thinking and worrying for the last two days, unable to decide how to handle a tricky family situation with my cousin. Not knowing what to do, I asked my Higher Power for help.

Just now, I made the decision. I picked up the phone, called her, and shared my concerns in a straightforward way. Everything turned out fine. I did the right thing.

Life is simple when I'm honest, open, and willing.

# JANUARY 30

# *In This Moment,*
# *I turn to God.*

I see how negative experiences in my childhood fed my codependence. My elders said, "Look what you made me do," "God will get you for this," and "Anger is not ladylike." I felt responsible for other people's happiness and feared God. I became a people-pleaser as I tried to be a good little girl.

Life experiences eventually led me to CoDA, where I learned that God is a constant, loving presence in my life. I keep in daily contact with God because this is what works for me. The message I receive is that I don't have to do or be anything special. I am enough just as I am.

# JANUARY 31

## *In This Moment, my nest is empty.*

I denied my needs for many years. I was too busy taking care of my loved ones.

Now, I have recovery and I take care of myself. In many instances, my Higher Power provides for me even before I am aware of my need. To me, this is amazing. I see the Twelfth Promise working: "I gradually experience serenity, strength, and spiritual growth in my daily life."

# FEBRUARY 1

## *In This Moment, snow falls.*

We face a major Nor'easter, which threatens to drop 20 or more inches of snow. I've been cooking all day because I always get the urge to cook and create during storms. The best days are when I don't have to go anywhere. My significant other has to work when it snows. A few years ago, I might have gone to work with him, and sat in my car with coffee and a book in order to avoid being home alone.

Today, I cherish my alone time. Why? I've learned in CoDA recovery to enjoy my own company. I know without a shadow of a doubt that I am never alone. My Higher Power is always present.

# FEBRUARY 2

## *In This Moment, I ask for help.*

Asking for help used to be so hard for me to do. I never asked. I didn't want to depend on anyone for fear that they might let me down or refuse to help me. I couldn't take that risk. I felt too vulnerable.

In recovery, I can ask for help, first from my Higher Power, and then from other people. I trust that help is available when I need it. I am no longer alone.

# FEBRUARY 3

# *In This Moment,*
# *I am healing.*

I am a recovering codependent. I am not stuck or doomed to be hopeless and helpless, forever repeating codependent patterns. I am growing. I don't need to be "fixed." I transform my past hurt and pain into gifts of deeper understanding and empathy. I am healing. I have hope for my future. As long as I breathe, I continue to recover and grow in this life. What a gift!

# FEBRUARY 4

## *In This Moment, I'm alone.*

I'm alone and that's OK. It's God's plan for me. I grew up surrounded by people, yet feeling lonely. Now, I get to finish growing up emotionally and spiritually. I am re-parenting myself by meeting my own needs. That means being the best me I can be. No more people-pleasing to gain acceptance. No more lies and cover-ups to meet someone else's needs. I use God's gifts, CoDA meetings, prayer and meditation, service work, exercise, affirmations, workshops, and more. Thanks, God. I feel better.

# FEBRUARY 5

## *In This Moment,*
## *I am learning who I am.*

No feelings were expressed in my house when I was growing up. Consequently, I learned not to feel. I developed several ways to keep my feelings down. I would get depressed instead of angry, anxious instead of scared or sad. If that didn't work, I'd overeat to stuff the feelings.

Now that I'm an adult in recovery, I'm learning it's OK to feel — but it's still hard. If I feel depressed and anxious, I still want to eat a box of cookies. What I've learned to do is identify those dysfunctional coping mechanisms as signals that I'm feeling something I need to deal with. I ask myself, "What am I feeling?" and then, "What do I need to do about it?" With the help of my meetings and Higher Power, I'm learning who I am.

# FEBRUARY 6

## *In This Moment, I ask, seek, and knock.*

When I ask, answers come.

When I seek, people cross my path.

When I knock, doors open.

I have new choices that bring change to my life, through new information, direction, and challenge. All of this is a gift of my working the Steps in CoDA. I now trust that my Higher Power will reveal to me all that I need to know.

# FEBRUARY 7

## *In This Moment, I'm in the best place.*

Every morning I start the day with a short meditation. One morning, I woke up feeling less than excited about the day. I allowed my thoughts to flow freely. I found myself going over the journey to where I am. I have been through hard times, but I have enjoyed good things, too. I would not be who I am today without the good and the bad.

I like who I am today. I am grateful for where the journey leads me. I am in the best place I can be.

# FEBRUARY 8

## *In This Moment, I ask for my Higher Power's help.*

When I feel anxious about something, when I am worried, when I want to control a situation so that it comes out the way I want, I ask my Higher Power for help. I ask, "Please help me with this. Help me to let go of the result. Help me to remember that it's your will be done, not mine. Help me to remember to 'let go and let God.'"

When I ask for God's help, it doesn't mean I get what I want. It means that what I get is what I need.

# FEBRUARY 9

# *In This Moment,*
# *I am deeply grateful to CoDA.*

CoDA offers me a safe space and the tools necessary to begin the healing process of recovery. Not every day is peaceful. Many are painful as I face and feel the frozen feelings from my past. Through the recovery process, which continually evolves, I gain greater ability to establish and maintain healthy and loving relationships, not only with others, but unexpectedly, and awesomely, with myself and my beloved Higher Power. Awareness of healing changes me within and leads me to gratitude, from which I derive strength and hope. In this moment, I am secure.

# FEBRUARY 10

# *In This Moment,*
# *I am spiritual.*

When my spirit is in harmony with life, I am renewed and refreshed with affirmation and wisdom. I have freedom to live without limitations and strength to bear all things. I am unique and precious. A surge of gladness travels throughout my being. I have hope for that which I once thought I could not accomplish. With grace, I find heaven within. I give thanks for the gifts of wonder, wholeness, and abundance.

# FEBRUARY 11

# *In This Moment, I must speak.*

It breaks my heart to take a stand that I fear will create turmoil. Yet, I must speak. Denying the truth has far worse consequences. Wellness for me is dependent on my ability to be honest. I am deeply grateful that I have a program which values honesty. By being true to myself, I can expect a miraculous change in my life. The fruits of the CoDA Promises are delicious!

# FEBRUARY 12

## *In This Moment, I feel young.*

As I gaze into the mirror, I envision myself looking radiant and beautiful, in a dress I have not worn for years.

At 65 years old, I am getting better every day! I am so thankful for my attitude in life. My faith in my Higher Power keeps my spirit young. I believe in the healing powers of my daily affirmations.

I haven't outgrown the curiosity of my youth. My curiosity led me to CoDA. Today, it is a joy in my life. I love the people I see there every week. They love me and accept me as I am.

# FEBRUARY 13

# *In This Moment, I'm growing.*

The divorce became final a year ago. It was a painful split. However, I have felt the pain and worked on letting it go. Today, my life has taken on new energy and I see a bright future. I still get twinges of pain when I walk through the men's department. I want to stop and browse and buy him something. I haven't looked at greeting cards for a long time. Recognizing these habits as triggers of pain has been a huge part of my growth. Instead of walking into a situation that will bring more pain, I make other choices. I change my thoughts as well. I know that I am being healed because the pain isn't so excruciating. Thanks to the Twelve Steps, I feel stronger and more serene.

# FEBRUARY 14

# *In This Moment, it's Valentine's Day.*

Although I was not promiscuous, I spent many Valentine's Days with different men. I find it hard to understand my behavior. My parents were happily married for over fifty years. Where did I learn that it was OK to leave a problematic relationship rather than to try to work it out? My fear of being alone drove me to hold onto failing relationships just long enough to look for the next one.

Today, in recovery, I enjoy my current relationship. I am willing to work through the ugly times that surface in any loving partnership. Today, I see a disagreement as an indication that I have some work to do, not as the signal to start looking for a replacement.

# FEBRUARY 15

## *In This Moment, I say goodbye to a wonderful vacation.*

I look out on the Caribbean Sea, trying to stamp this view into my memory. I'm going home and I love my home. Still, I feel sad to leave this place and the good friends who invited me here. Transitions are stressful even when I like where I'm going. At one time, transition was from terror and despair to eventual peace and hope.

Thanks to my Higher Power, today I go from one good thing to another. My life and my decisions are my own; with my Higher Power's help, I know everything is going to be OK.

# FEBRUARY 16

## *In This Moment, I'm sewing up my coat.*

I stopped by an ATM on the way to visit a doctor. On returning to my car, I couldn't locate my keys. I went back to the ATM. No keys. I gingerly checked the car doors. All were locked. Inside the car were my pocketbook with the extra key, my gloves, and my cell phone. Just as I was about to panic, a little voice reminded me that my big coat has a hole in the pocket. Sure enough, my keys had slipped through the hole down to the hem area. Higher Power saved the day!

# FEBRUARY 17

# *In This Moment,*
# *I mind my own business.*

I'm grateful for the CoDA program. I've learned that by allowing others to live their own lives, I have the time and energy to tend to my own affairs. I once thought I was helping others by doing things for them. I gave them a silent message that I thought they weren't capable of doing for themselves. I gained a false sense of importance, but avoided real growth opportunities. As a result, their self-esteem suffered and so did mine.

Now, I'm aware that my relationships with others improve when I mind only my business. My good feelings about myself increase as I work through my own issues. I always have plenty to do!

# FEBRUARY 18

## *In This Moment, gratitude works.*

A few years ago, I read a book that said the best prayer is a gratitude prayer. Since that day, my prayers always start with, "Thank you, God." It works! When I lost my job, I started a daily prayer thanking God for the new job I knew would come. Despite my being unemployed, I had serenity because I was confident in my Higher Power's will for me. Today, I have the best job I ever had. Thank you, God.

# FEBRUARY 19

## *In This Moment, I let go of past negative beliefs.*

My negativity used to stop me from loving myself and loving others. Now, when old beliefs creep into my thought patterns, I remember the work I have done on Step Four. I remind myself of how much I have grown in recovery. I stop, own my behavior, and make positive changes.

Through experiencing change, I know in my heart that all is possible. When I realize that negativity is seeping into my thinking, I know that I have a choice to let go of old ways. If I am taking someone else's inventory, or taking my own, I remind myself that we are all children of God. Each one of us deserves to be treated with love and respect.

# FEBRUARY 20

## *In This Moment, I have spirituality.*

My life was unmanageable. I had no goals, no insights. I struggled with decision-making. Before CoDA, I had religion. Now, I have spirituality which sustains me on a daily basis. I have a Higher Power to guide, support, and listen to me. My spirituality and Higher Power have lifted a great burden from my shoulders. I no longer have to do anything alone.

# FEBRUARY 21

## *In This Moment, I'm God's child.*

I'm beautiful as is. I don't need to change to please the world. I continue to grow, at my own pace, in peace and understanding. I am no longer lost as before. Now, I have a Fellowship which understands and cares about me. I can talk things over with my sponsor. I don't have to face my feelings alone. I have friends to talk to and do things with — and I have a Higher Power who never lets me down.

# FEBRUARY 22

## *In This Moment, I have choices.*

I don't have to live from the script where I play the victim. I can write my script in a way that is healthy for me. I am now more likely to evaluate the situation as it is happening, calmly view the options available to me, and make a choice. I have the freedom to improvise. I am living the most perfect life I am capable of living. I am happy, healthy, and making progress every day.

# FEBRUARY 23

# *In This Moment,*
# *I feel sane and serene.*

The first time I faced Step Two, I had trouble believing that a Higher Power could change my life. Yet I saw lives that had been transformed. In the rooms, I heard people share that their lives had once been as desolate as mine. Yet they seemed to have something that I did not. I came to believe that whatever caused the change in them could cause the same changes in me. At first, I made my Twelve Step group my Higher Power. This gave me a start. As time went by and I progressed through the Twelve Steps, I began to notice that I was changing. I came to believe in a power greater than myself — and I found serenity.

# FEBRUARY 24

## *In This Moment, I love life.*

It wasn't always so. After my husband died, I wrote a book about our marriage from the wedding to his death. I included everything I could remember, the bad as well as the good. In the year since I finished, I have gone back to reread it. I found that I left out a lot of the happy times. I was there but not there. I spent so much time thinking and talking about past resentments, and projecting potential problems, that I was sleepwalking through the present.

Today, I live in the present. I like who I am and where I am. I enjoy each day and get the most out of it. I will never lose myself again. That's why I keep going to CoDA meetings and reading CoDA literature. Thanks to CoDA, I have a life today.

# FEBRUARY 25

## *In This Moment, a new way is better.*

The lack of attention and preponderance of "No" from Mom in childhood is countered with equal intensity of not accepting the "No" and needing the "Yes" from my intimate partner. The needier I am, the more I set myself up for rejection. Now that I've been hit in the gut with that awareness, I can figure out how to change.

The truth is that the old way doesn't work. The new way is better. First, I recognize that I have a problem and then, with the help of my Higher Power, I begin to work to correct it. How blessed I am to have the Twelve Steps as a guide on how to live life.

# FEBRUARY 26

# *In This Moment,*
# *I have healthy relationships.*

I first came to CoDA to learn how to have healthier love relationships. I had just been dumped by my partner, who was everything to me.

CoDA changed my life in more ways than just my love life. I learned how to have healthier relationships with my parents, my siblings, and others. I learned I didn't have to live in fear of my boss, that I could ask for help or more time or whatever I needed. I even have healthier three-minute relationships with cashiers.

As time went on, I realized these people hadn't changed; I had. Rather than having to change the world to fit my vision for it, I could adjust my vision to see the beauty in the world. The greatest change occurred in my relationship with myself. I have peace and serenity.

# FEBRUARY 27

## *In This Moment,*
## *I love myself.*

Even if I do not feel loving, I act as if I love myself. I get enough rest and exercise. I provide healthy, nutritious food for my body. I listen to my inner self. I nurture it and give it what it needs to heal. I stimulate my mind to learn and try new things. I listen to my spirit for the wisdom in its quiet voice and subtle guidance. I allow my genuine self to shine through and my masks to fall away. I am whole. I am me. I am.

# **FEBRUARY 28**

## *In This Moment,*
## *I choose how to spend my time.*

Although other people and situations may pressure me, ultimately I make the decision of how to spend my time. Not making a choice is a choice. How I spend my minutes, hours, and days determines how I live my life. Am I living the life I want to lead? Or am I living the way someone else thinks I should? Sometimes in order to say "yes" to what I want, I have to say "no" to something else. If I spend time figuring out what's really important to me, I can focus my energy on those areas. Knowing what's important to me helps me achieve my goals and enjoy life.

# **FEBRUARY 29**

## *In This Moment,*
## *I live my own life.*

Lately, I'm not allowing myself to be pulled into other people's business. This is a good sign of my recovery! Meddling is a codependent trait that I am trying to change. People ask me to solve their problems. Although I'm tempted, I choose to say, "No." It's enabling if I rescue them. Either they find the courage to do it themselves or they suffer the consequences. I have my own life to live. It's better for me to take care of my own business and better for others, too.

# MARCH 1

## *In This Moment, I have hope.*

When I was little, I had lots of dreams for a life of happiness. Somewhere along the way, I gave up on those dreams. My life was full of problems. I believed that my problems were all someone else's fault.

By working my program and going to CoDA meetings, I learned that my life is what I make of it. Now, I have hope. I see ice, snow, and grayness out my window. But in just a few weeks I'll be looking at fresh green grass, pink roses, and golden sunshine. Seasons change and so will I.

# MARCH 2

## *In This Moment,*
## *I live in the moment.*

Only memories remain. No matter what my past contains, it's gone. I can't change the past, what I did, or what happened to me. My past is part of me — I can learn from it and focus on the present. Each day is a new chapter. It's up to me to fill it.

With my Higher Power's guidance, I choose to let go of the pain and hurt of the past. I embrace my future, trusting it to the care of God. I honor myself in the present.

# MARCH 3

## *In This Moment, my Higher Power cares for me.*

"To the care of God" (Step Three) means that my Higher Power really cares about me. I'm turning my life and my will over to one who cares for me more than I cared for myself.

Believing that my Higher Power protects and directs me was a giant leap of faith. Once I made the leap and became willing, my Higher Power started working in my life.

# MARCH 4

# *In This Moment,*
# *I feel nurtured.*

I like this new feeling. I never felt nurtured as a kid. I am powerless over others, but I have choices.

Today, in recovery, I choose to be with healthy people. I spent the day with others in recovery. I spent the evening with CoDA friends. I'm taking care of myself by choosing to be with caring people. Thanks to CoDA, I am healthy enough to make that choice.

# MARCH 5

# *In This Moment,*
# *I am powerless over others.*

I can badger, persuade, manipulate, cajole, shame, control, withhold, resent, or bully others. Is there power in such attempts? The answer is, "No." Recognizing that my life is unmanageable and experiencing chaos are clues that I am trying to seek power. What insanity to pursue this. But how familiar this subtle, habitual obsession is to me.

Step One is both the hope and the beginning of my spiritual solution. Working this Step allows me to identify, accept, and admit that I am powerless over others. What a relief!

# MARCH 6

# *In This Moment, I am honest with myself.*

Honesty means finding freedom through truthfulness. When I get in touch with my true feelings, I dig deeper to the root cause of my dysfunction. In Step Four, my personal inventory uncovers my character defects. In Step Five, I work with my sponsor and Higher Power to plant the seeds of healing, where once there was disease. Where there was turmoil, now there is serenity. Once tormented by fear, now I have courage. Ignorance and foolishness have been replaced with wisdom. All of this happens when I do my part and allow God to do God's part.

# MARCH 7

# *In This Moment, I imagine.*

Imagination makes dreams a reality,

A glorious world of outstanding beauty,

A consciousness of inner glory.

Kind words abound in absolute caring,

Encouragement and enrichment flow to peace.

An unyielding challenge brings confidence,

Not doubt or denial, but hope for new life in recovery.

# MARCH 8

## *In This Moment, I learn the most important thing.*

I am grateful for my life today. When I came into recovery, I was newly separated. I was desperate to find someone who could give my life purpose — someone I could take care of, my soul mate. I heard at meetings that recovery meant learning how to take care of me, how to love myself. I didn't have a clue. I never learned that concept. Through working my program, I learned the most important lesson: "I am all I need." Today, I can say, "I like me, I really like me!"

# MARCH 9

## *In This Moment,*
## *I choose to take care of myself.*

When I feel out of control and my stomach is tied in knots, I stop, breathe, and remember that I have many tools to handle any situation. I remind myself that I am capable of taking care of me. I make good, smart decisions about my life. I trust that my Higher Power always provides guidance and direction, help and safety, love and joy. I just need to become quiet to get in touch with that strength. I know it is present in my life.

# MARCH 10

# *In This Moment, I ask my Higher Power for the willingness to make amends.*

Sometimes, I'm not ready to make amends. I've learned that it's rarely beneficial to wait to make amends. Procrastination is fear of failure. I ask myself, "Failure of what? It's an amends. The response of the other person is irrelevant." I see that the only failure is the failure to make the amends. I'm feeling reluctant, so I ask my Higher Power for help. When I ask God for the courage and willingness to walk through it, and I do it, I always feel better. That's when I see that the CoDA Promises do come true.

# MARCH 11

# *In This Moment,*
# *I follow God's will for me.*

I'm learning to let go and it feels good not to be in charge all the time. I have boundless energy to do my will, but often procrastinate on important issues. For too long, I hung to the end of a rope with no clear understanding of the meaning of life. Through prayer, I'm redirecting my energy to know and do God's will. It's comforting to know that I don't have to carry the full load anymore. I know what it means to be happy, joyous, and free. The amazing thing is that the plans of my Higher Power far exceed anything I could have imagined.

# MARCH 12

# *In This Moment,*
# *I don't take myself so seriously.*

At my first CoDA meeting, I couldn't understand why all those people were smiling and laughing. Didn't they know life is serious? My problems were overwhelming and I thought recovery had to be serious work. Some people invited me to join them for coffee after the meeting. There they poked fun at themselves. In time, I realized how terribly "humor impaired" I had become. I wanted what they had. Gradually, I joined the mirth and merriment.

Today, I can laugh. Now, it's my turn to invite a newcomer to join us for coffee. And joy of joys, I am being restored to sanity.

# MARCH 13

# *In This Moment,*
# *I am worthy of recovery.*

I was having trouble with my recovery. I hadn't called my sponsor for a while or done any writing. I stopped reading recovery books. I felt I wasn't working my program well and was ashamed to go to meetings. Fortunately, I remembered Tradition Three: "The only requirement for membership in CoDA is a desire for healthy and loving relationships." I realized what mattered was that I still desired that. A CoDA meeting isn't just a place for me to talk about how I've recovered. It's a place for me to learn how to recover. When I feel unworthy is when I really need a meeting.

# MARCH 14

## *In This Moment, I need meetings.*

As I was sitting in a CoDA meeting the other night, slowly feeling better as folks shared, it suddenly struck me — for the hundredth time — how indispensable meetings are in my recovery. I need to be in meetings regularly to keep my disease at bay. I need to hear people talking about taking care of themselves, and I need to share my recovery with others. I need to hear over and over that I have a right to take care of myself, that my Higher Power is within me — not in people, places, and things. Today, in my new life, I am so grateful I have healthy meetings that I can attend regularly. I need 'em.

# MARCH 15

## *In This Moment, I'm happy in my home sweet home.*

I'm sitting on my screen porch enjoying a beautiful morning with blue skies and wifty little clouds. The trees and grass are so green; the red hibiscus is blooming. The birds are singing and my dog and cat are next to me. It's so good to be home in the south, where nearly all days start like this. For the last three mornings, I've been up north at a CoDA get-together, where there is still ice on the river and trees are bare. The locals were delighted with temperatures in the 50's and 60's, but to me that's winter. Travel is fun, but there is no place like home.

# MARCH 16

# *In This Moment,*
# *I get the message.*

Years ago, before CoDA, I cross-stitched some sayings to hang on my kitchen wall. While I was stitching them, I thought about how much these sayings would help my husband see some of the behaviors I thought he needed to change.

After I'd attended CoDA meetings for a while, I looked at those wall hangings and realized that whether or not they helped my husband, they were all things I needed to look at in myself. Thanks to recovery, I finally get the message! If there's something I feel someone else needs to know or understand, maybe I'm the one who needs to hear it.

# MARCH 17

# *In This Moment, being right is not enough.*

When I am about to open my mouth to justify my response, when I am about to raise my voice in reaction to a statement, or when I feel my pulse quicken and the tears start welling up, I need to take a deep breath and call on my Higher Power for help. Sometimes, in my need to be right, I forget the greater purpose of learning to change my behaviors. I need to ask myself, "How important is it?" Often, the answer is obvious. The solution lies in my acceptance of things being just the way they are meant to be in this moment. I remind myself to "Let go and let God."

# MARCH 18

## *In This Moment, I live in reality.*

Living in reality is a habit I need to cultivate. I made a list of promises to myself. The first was, "See reality, accept reality." This promise has become a strong part of who I am today. Sometimes, I find myself lost in daydreams, reinventing the past, and wondering about the future. Fantasy has felt familiar, safe, and comfortable. Now, I believe that the temporary pleasure of fantasizing puts me on a deceptive path that's hard to leave. As quickly as possible, I work to replace fantasy with healthier thoughts. A firm footing in reality is a gift.

# MARCH 19

# *In This Moment,*
# *I strive for clarity.*

I realize that with nearly every positive statement I make, I add "but." I don't know why I do this. I think I may be afraid to say the negative without first making a positive statement. I may be afraid to tell you I don't like something, so I sneak it in with a compliment. I've justified this practice by saying that it's more honest to present both sides of an issue. I'm aware that by not making clear statements, I give mixed messages and avoid taking responsibility for my feelings. This is an issue for me to work on as I continue on my recovery journey.

# MARCH 20

# *In This Moment,*
# *I feel relieved.*

Yesterday, I made a mistake. I hurt someone's feelings. Thinking about it on my way home, I felt terrible. Thoughts tumbled over one another in my head. I wasn't sure, but maybe I needed to make amends. I called my sponsor and we discussed it. I also asked my Higher Power for guidance. The answer was clear. Step Nine. I made the amends. I said I was sorry. Doing Step Nine took the whole mess out of my head. This was not an experience I wanted to repeat and I told myself I wouldn't make the same mistake again.

# MARCH 21

# *In This Moment,*
# *I enjoy spring.*

I see spring as a time of rebirth when the whole world seems to have been renewed. In the north, new leaves, pretty flowers, and occasional warm days emerge. Here in Florida, where I live, it means less traffic, swimming days, and warm evenings out on the porch. It's a time to reflect upon my life, and the changes I want to make, as I continue growing and healing. I feel energized and renewed.

# MARCH 22

# *In This Moment, I see and believe.*

I attended a retreat this year in a beautiful lodge nestled on a mountaintop. Although people around me talked about the wonderful view, I was unable to see it because of the foggy weather. My recovery was like that at first. People told their stories of recovery. I heard how my view of life would change by working the Steps. I couldn't see it at first; all I could see was the fog. I slowly began to recognize the obvious recovery of others in my group. I worked the Steps and slowly but steadily, the fog lifted. Now, I reverse the old saying, "seeing is believing" into "believing leads to seeing."

# MARCH 23

# *In This Moment, I'm a happy codependent.*

Despite being codependent, I'm happy within my own skin. I have friends in the Fellowship who have a great sense of humor and positive outlook on life. They get it. I think that's because they are able to let go and let God. They're good role models for me. I want to see the glass half full. I want to get rid of fear. I work my program, do service, sponsor, and have a sponsor. I am happy because CoDA gives me so much.

# MARCH 24

# *In This Moment, I speak up.*

Growing up in a home where caretaking and enmeshment were the norm, where peace at any price was the unspoken rule, I learned to stuff my feelings. Today, when a loved one speaks to me in a demeaning or abusive tone, I have choices. In my mind, I sort out the incident and focus on my responsibility, my reaction, my feelings. I ask myself, "What is my part in this situation? What do I need to do to take care of myself?"

Today, through working the Twelve Steps of Co-Dependents Anonymous, I have found my voice. I no longer stay silent in order to keep the peace. I share my feelings and ask for what I need. I speak up.

# MARCH 25

## *In This Moment, my feelings just are.*

I'm feeling some painful emotions. I know from experience that I can survive and come out stronger on the other side. My feelings do not have to make sense or be logical or have a good reason for being. They just are.

The first step in making sense of my feelings is to identify them. My part is to be honest and acknowledge my feelings. I bring them out into the light. God takes care of the rest.

# MARCH 26

# *In This Moment,*
# *I'm making lemonade.*

Many years ago, a friend gave me a banner that said, "When life gives you lemons, make lemonade." I admire that positive attitude. I've had some "lemons" in my life. When I adopt an attitude of gratitude, they become benefits. I know there is something good for me in every situation. I just need to be aware in order to find it.

# MARCH 27

# *In This Moment, I set boundaries.*

I never knew about boundaries until I came into recovery. I had none, but I wanted some. The other day, one of my friends wanted to gossip about someone else's problems. I told her, "That's really none of my business" and changed the subject. Last week, my mother asked me to arrange a dinner for my ex and our two grown sons. I told her, "If they want to do it, they can arrange it for themselves." I set boundaries and stuck to them. What growth!

# MARCH 28

# *In This Moment,*
# *my eyes are open.*

Some mornings, I don't want to get up and I don't. I lie in bed, comfy but cheerless. I don't want to start the day. When I have an appointment, I stay in bed until the last possible second before getting up and dressed and out the door. I have followed this pattern since I was a depressed little girl.

In this moment, on a spring morning, I'm out of bed! I'm surprised — I'm aware — even hopeful. I'm enjoying a bit of spring sun peeking through my windows. Thank you, Higher Power, for opening my eyes.

# MARCH 29

# *In This Moment, I'm afraid.*

I spend a lot of time looking for my glasses and keys. Just now, I missed my doctor's appointment because I was mistaken about the time. I don't seem to absorb or retain new information very well. Friends tell me they're forgetful, too, but I fear I'm not just absent-minded.

I don't want this fear to dominate my life. I remind myself that I'm powerless over the outcome. For help, I focus on CoDA's Promise: "I am no longer controlled by my fears."

# MARCH 30

## *In This Moment, I accept God's will for me.*

I no longer pray for specific outcomes of events for others and myself. I remember that I am responsible for the action and God is in charge of the outcome. It's God's will, not mine, that will prevail. The more I'm in touch with seeing God's will for me, the more willing I am to accept it in my life. As I bring my will in line with God's will for me, I'm more at peace in this world, no matter what's going on outside me.

# MARCH 31

## *In This Moment, I am responsible for my actions.*

No matter how others act towards me, I am responsible for my actions. I do not have to take on their fear or their stuff. No one can make me feel anything that I don't choose to believe. Someone's criticism or bad behavior is a gift that I can decline or accept. I may respond in ways that respect myself and the other person or simply walk away. I take time to examine constructive criticism and determine if there's a nugget of truth to it. If there is, I take action to make positive changes in my life. If there is no truth to it, I let it go.

# APRIL 1

## *In This Moment,*
## *I speak up for myself.*

Even if I'm uncomfortable, I speak up when another person's behavior bothers me. I no longer fear speaking my mind or telling others when I feel uncomfortable. If I am not at ease about how I'm being treated, I speak directly, clearly, and concisely. I do my part by expressing my feelings clearly. I tell others specifically what I like instead of forcing them to play a guessing game. The more I practice speaking up and being honest, the easier it gets.

**APRIL 2**

# *In This Moment, I am grateful for little miracles.*

I'm so grateful for the Twelve Steps, which have opened my eyes to the little miracles in my life. All that's required is my willingness to slow down when life in the fast lane gets too rough. I used to try to work harder and faster.

Today, I slow down so I can enjoy the little miracles God sends my way. The cardinal on my windowsill, that parking space in front when I'm running late, a call from a special friend, or just a few unexpected moments to myself on a hectic day – these are the little miracles I see when I take the time to look. They're all around me when I open my eyes and my heart.

**APRIL 3**

# *In This Moment, I'm working on my list.*

I feel overwhelmed. Step Eight asks me to make a list of all those I have harmed. There are so many people to include. I don't know if I'll be able to make amends to them all. I've lost contact with many; some are deceased.

My focus is drawn to the last part of this Step, "became willing to make amends to them all." There's my answer. I don't have to figure out how to make amends. Not today. What I need to do now is finish my list and become willing. With my Higher Power's help, I can do this!

# APRIL 4

## *In This Moment, I let go of my anger.*

I let God do for me what I can not do for myself. My father was a rageaholic. Anger also came easily to his wife and child; it was second nature to me. In my Sixth Step work, God acted on my behalf, taking me at my word that I was ready to have this character defect removed. I am now more even-tempered and pleasant than I ever imagined possible. I interact with people in a productive way, without getting caught up in emotional crossfire. I focus on principles before personalities. I let God lead the way.

# APRIL 5

## *In This Moment, life is good.*

I'm so grateful. Recently I made many changes in my life: new job, new home, new state. I can take credit for some, but not all. I didn't do it alone. My Higher Power was with me every step of the way. I received many signs assuring me I was doing the right thing. Some of them got my attention like a bolt out of the blue. I smile as I remember how clear the message was. I am on a journey. There are bumps in the road, sure, but where it has taken me is truly amazing.

# APRIL 6

## *In This Moment, I ask God how I might be of service today.*

Step Twelve reminds me that I can only keep what I've received from the program of Co-Dependents Anonymous by continually giving it away. This is one of the great paradoxes of the program. Sponsorship is one form of Twelve Step work that I have chosen. Working with others is rewarding and enlightening. I discover which of my character defects needs attention through the process of interacting with another codependent in recovery. Being a single parent means I have to set limits on the time I spend with sponsees. If I don't, I become frazzled and my family suffers. Then I'm not good to anyone. By taking care of myself, I have more energy to give to others.

# APRIL 7

## *In This Moment, I'm lighthearted.*

I am prone to melancholia. If I don't stay connected to my Higher Power, I lose serenity and slip into depression. When I consciously look for signs or answers, I find delightful, everyday surprises which keep me grateful and positive. The other morning as I was dragging myself into work, thinking unkind thoughts about my boss, a bird sang out the universal "pretty girl" whistle. At first I thought it was one of my students being a wise guy. When I looked again, there was the blackbird sitting atop a light pole, whistling! I laughed out loud and said "Thank you!" The rest of the day, I was more lighthearted.

# APRIL 8

## *In This Moment, I feel compassion.*

For a long time, my heart was small and blocked. I didn't feel compassion for others or myself. Then my Higher Power awakened in me the capacity to feel compassion. Now, I feel no need to judge or fix others. I have no reason to feel pity or rush them through their pain. Compassion allows me to sit with a friend and listen. In such moments, I feel compassion for myself as well as my friend.

When I listen with my heart, I hear beyond mere words and into the heart of another human being. Compassion is an awe-inspiring gift from God.

# APRIL 9

## *In This Moment, I remind myself "progress, not perfection."*

Doing a Fourth Step is like peeling an onion, one layer at a time. Before program, I excused my character defects as "just who I am." I've now worked two Fourth Step inventories. My sponsor said quite cheerfully that I'd be lucky to uncover even 40% of my character defects. I thought someone as intelligent as I am could surely uncover everything the first time. My sponsor was right. Early in my recovery, I couldn't see the character defects I recognize today. Likewise, there are defects I'm not ready to acknowledge today. They will be revealed when I'm ready. I do the footwork by taking daily inventories and staying aware of my behaviors. I'm making progress.

# APRIL 10

## *In This Moment, I'm free to be me.*

When I find myself struggling to be who I am, I think back to who I was when I first came to CoDA. I believed I had no character faults. I grew up being whatever everyone else wanted me to be. I had no sense of who I was. When I read CoDA's patterns of codependency about denial, low self-esteem, and control, I knew I was "home." It was as if someone had written my life story. Today, if I find myself in a situation where I am tempted to act in a way that no longer fits, I have the freedom to act differently. Old patterns, like old clothes, don't fit anymore. I have choices. I can decide to act in a healthy manner. I feel free.

# APRIL 11

## *In This Moment, I change the CD.*

Today, a part of me wants to stay in bed. What if I could imagine how it would be to wake up happy, joyous, and free. Oh! What a gift that would be. Yeah, but here I am just lying here, a little down and tired of the same ol' same ol'. Hey! Snap out of it! The sun is coming up, the birds are singing, the breeze is gently rustling the leaves, the sky is blue, and I get a new chance to make this a happy day.

Yes, it is my choice. Do I choose self-pity or do I choose happiness? I can get up and put a new CD in my head. CD could be Change Day. Yes! Today I change the message. I'm happy to be alive.

# APRIL 12

## *In This Moment, I forgive myself.*

After ten years of recovery, I am in pain again. I need to do another Fourth Step. Out comes the pen and paper. Out comes anger, pain, and resentments. And finally, out come some character defects that I have worn like armor all my life. How could I be so blind?

Talking to my sponsor helps me realize that God has brought me to this point in my life. When I become entirely ready, God shows me the way.

## APRIL 13

# *In This Moment,*
# *I am where I need to be.*

Right now, I'm taking a moment to stop my usual pinball reactions to life. I'm pausing to reflect on where I am. I feel my feelings. A little tired…relaxed…now calmer…a touch of gratitude for the tool of self-awareness, knowing I can own my power. I'm owning it right now. I stop to check in with myself and see what's up or what's down. I know it's all OK. If I'm here for myself, I can never be abandoned. I promise myself, in this moment, to stay on my own side. That's where I need to be.

# APRIL 14

## *In This Moment, I find things I like.*

I lift my head, look around, and see a beautiful fuchsia color on the cover of a notebook. I like that. I look out the window and see the bright green in a patch of new spring grass. Wow! I like that. I see my children all cozy and asleep, peaceful and trusting. My Higher Power put these little people and me together in this world. I like that.

Everything else in my life may be total chaos, but I can look up from where I am and know that I am here, and this is who I am meant to be. I like that a lot.

# APRIL 15

# *In This Moment,*
# *I know gratitude.*

Negative thinking was my family's trait. Whatever the situation, I could imagine the worst possible outcome. It could be a sunny day, with but a single cloud, and someone in my family would conclude it was going to rain. When called to my boss's office, I always feared I'd be fired.

For a while after I got into CoDA recovery, my financial situation worsened. My savings were gone. I was unemployed. There was only one more unemployment check. I envisioned myself homeless, sleeping under a highway overpass. At that point, God changed my thinking. I began to look for things about which I could be grateful. I find at least three things for which I am grateful every day. Some of the CoDA Promises started to come true for me. It happened the moment gratitude became part of my daily life.

# APRIL 16

## *In This Moment, I admit I make mistakes.*

I hate making mistakes. I try to do things "right," but when I find myself in a complete rat's nest of my own making, I feel devastated. I used to try to cover up a mistake, deny it, or punish myself for it (before anyone else got a chance). Now, I have a better choice. I practice Step Ten and simply admit it. I made a mistake, but I am still OK. I accept my own imperfection and embrace my humanity. This way "I release myself from worry, guilt, and regret about my past" (Promise Four) and move forward.

# APRIL 17

## *In This Moment, I choose not to listen.*

The committee in my head shouts at me that I'm unworthy, inadequate, not good enough. It's replaying dialogue from the past. The committee is old; it's been there for a long time. I think it's time it retired.

I'm replacing it with positive affirmations. I have CoDA's affirmation booklet on my nightstand. Every morning, I open it and randomly choose one. That becomes my mantra for the day. I do this so the committee can't pull a sneak attack.

# APRIL 18

# *In This Moment, I am present.*

I am here. I notice all the gifts around me that my Higher Power places in my life. I slow down enough to see all the bright colors in my surroundings. I do not judge whether things "should" or "should not" be. When it rains, I let the raindrops fall on my face and experience them fully. When the sun shines, I soak up its rays. My Higher Power has given me a place in this wondrous universe.

# APRIL 19

# *In This Moment,*
# *I am enough.*

I am the sum of all my yesterdays. I am this moment's thoughts, actions, and feelings. I relish being in the moment. I thank my Higher Power for leading me to the CoDA program and showing me a path out of insanity. The love I feel for myself and others fills my heart and my soul. I am enough.

# **APRIL 20**

## *In This Moment, I let go of expectations.*

When I was new in the CoDA program, I called my sponsor to complain. She replied with one word: Expectations. She was right. My unrealistic expectations of somebody else's behavior caused turmoil. On some occasions, it was caused by unrealistic expectations of my own behavior. People are who they are and they do what they do. I am not here on earth to be their judge. I'll be OK as long as I expect people to be themselves, not who I want them to be.

# APRIL 21

# *In This Moment, I gain trust.*

When I'm scared, upset, or lack clarity about a situation with another person, I remember I am not helpless or alone. I am not a victim. Growing up in a home where healthy conflict resolution was never modeled and where emotional neglect was the norm, I came to doubt that I could take care of myself.

Learning to trust is a process. As I attend meetings and work the Twelve Steps with my sponsor, I gain more trust that my Higher Power will give me peace, regardless of the circumstances. Today, when I am in turmoil, I stop for a moment and rest in the safe haven of my Higher Power.

# APRIL 22

## *In This Moment, I choose self-worth.*

I remove toxic people, situations, substances, and behaviors from my life. I replace the old messages with new supportive, healthy ones. I develop new behaviors that nurture my growth. I listen to my feelings and use them as a tool and guide. I choose to change because I no longer wish to repeat the same old behaviors. I am learning my lessons. I am growing. I am developing self-worth. I deserve good things in my life and create my own happiness.

# **APRIL 23**

# *In This Moment, I stand my ground.*

My boundary has been violated. What do I do? It took all the courage I had just to set it. I spent hours in support groups to find the courage to state it. I found my power. I spoke my truth. I stated my limit. I trusted God.

Now, someone is stomping all over it. Can I stand my ground? This is a test: Can I defend my boundary now that I've set it? Oh yes! With my Higher Power's help I can. This is "walking through the fire." There are gems of wisdom to be found in the ashes.

# APRIL 24

## *In This Moment, I reach out for help.*

I share my feelings and experiences with others. I pick up the phone and call my sponsor or another person in recovery. Someone else may have gone through a similar experience and understand what I'm going through. Often, I do not need advice; I just need to be heard. I am responsible for my own life, but I do not have to do everything alone. When I need someone to be there for me, I ask. I am not alone.

# APRIL 25

# *In This Moment,*
# *I take my inventory.*

Lots of times I focus on other people's faults. It's easier than facing my own. Today, I'm taking my own inventory. Often, I find it hard to speak up for myself. I let other people control me. I have put their peace of mind ahead of mine. My peace of mind is important to me. I have to do what's best for me. I have said, "No, thank you." And, "I have other plans." And, "That's not good for me right now." Life is too short to live any other way.

# APRIL 26

# *In This Moment,*
# *I trust myself.*

In my childhood, breaches of trust seriously impacted my self-esteem and ability to trust my gut instincts. I grew up thinking I was supposed to trust others automatically. When others broke that trust, I was confused and upset. I wondered what I had done wrong to cause them to be dishonest.

I've learned in CoDA that I'm not responsible for others. People need to earn trust, and some people just aren't worthy of trust. I let go of relationships with people I can't trust. Today, I choose to share my life with trustworthy people.

# APRIL 27

## *In This Moment, I look in the mirror and see myself.*

It never occurred to me to make amends to myself while looking into a mirror, as the book *Co-Dependents Anonymous* suggests. Before CoDA, when I looked in a mirror, I saw a person, but I never saw myself. A friend in my Step study group mentioned doing a Fifth Step in front of a mirror. When I did, I touched some of my self-abandonment, self-neglect, and self-abuse issues. The transformation was amazing. I saw <u>me</u>, who I really am, and I fully accepted myself. What a powerful experience.

# APRIL 28

# *In This Moment, I just do it!*

I'm working to gain confidence in my ability to make the right decisions and to say the right things at the right times. I believe the answers are within me, so I wonder why I don't trust myself at times. Friends and family encourage me, God believes in me, and yet I often doubt their good opinion. Why don't I believe in me? For one day, I'll ignore my shame, fear, and doubts — and just do it.

# APRIL 29

## *In This Moment, I recognize that conflict can be good.*

As a codependent, controversy and conflict are things that I have often preferred to avoid. Working through these uncomfortable feelings, with the help of my sponsor, I've learned there are healthy ways to address issues. I practice my new behaviors within the CoDA program. If I don't like the way meetings are held, literature is distributed, or group monies spent, I can ask for and participate in a group conscience. Things don't always go my way, but I feel good that my opinions are heard. Today, I view conflict and controversy as opportunities for growth.

# APRIL 30

## *In This Moment,*
## *I am lovable, loving, and loved.*

Sometimes my heart feels closed. I can't feel the love that others, including my Higher Power, have for me.

In recovery, I learn to trust. When I open myself up in safety, my heart opens as well. I realize I am lovable. This love expands over time, and through my Higher Power, I feel a passion for my friends and family that I never felt before. I am loving. When I feel the love others have for me, I realize I am loved.

# MAY 1

## *In This Moment, I am willing to change.*

In the past, I thought my life would be better if other people changed. But that didn't happen and I was miserable. I came to CoDA hoping to learn how to change other people. What a surprise to find out that I was the one who had to change! Now, when I say the *Serenity Prayer,* I concentrate on "the wisdom to know the difference." If I stop, think, and pray, I discover choices. Change begins with me. Today, I'm willing.

# MAY 2

# *In This Moment, I am.*

I exist. I am no longer a cringing shadow in the corner. I am substantial. I have a presence. I have personality, character, and personal style. I matter. I am free to be me, up front and in the open. I am an integral part of the universe. I am needed. I am here to fulfill my purpose on this earth. I am unique. I am precious. I am me.

# MAY 3

## *In This Moment, I start anew.*

Before recovery, I spent many years hiding, never being honest with anyone — family, friends, co-workers, myself, and most of all, God. I didn't even know I was being dishonest. All of my self-centeredness, self-pity, and self-will had to go. As a result of working the Third Step, I surrendered my will and my life over to God. I am grateful for my recovery and the changes I have made. I'm a new person. I thank God, because now I know what it means to start anew.

# MAY 4

# *In This Moment, I feel heard.*

Prior to going to CoDA meetings, the "no talk" rule was a big part of my life. Talking about the weather, sports, or the kids was permitted. Talking about my feelings or insecurities was forbidden. Because of my profession, no one wanted to hear that I had problems. Even among colleagues, I didn't feel safe. I feared that if they really knew me, they would shun me.

It's safe to talk in CoDA meetings. Sharing is healing for me. When I led a meeting, I told the ugly story of my moral, personal, and professional failures. People didn't shun me; they gave me hugs. They appreciated my honesty and urged me to "keep coming back." I'm going to, because at meetings my outside matches my inside and it feels good. Now, when I need to be heard and accepted, I find a CoDA meeting.

# MAY 5

# *In This Moment, I see good as well as bad.*

Step Four asks that I take a "searching and fearless moral inventory." When making a personal inventory, I include my good points and bad — those behaviors I value as well as those I wish to change. Even if I'm not sure if a behavior is good or bad, I write it down anyway. My sponsor may have some valuable insight when it comes time to do my Fifth Step. The hardest part of doing my inventory is breaking through denial. I can't inventory something I don't know exists. Once I'm aware of a behavior, I'm usually willing to write it down, share it, and ask that my defect be removed. Getting there takes time and that's OK with me today.

# MAY 6

## *In This Moment, I am grateful for meetings.*

After almost eleven years, I keep coming back to meetings. Sometimes, I wonder why. Not many people stay around that long. It seems like whenever I think about not going to meetings, my Higher Power hits me with some kind of crisis — sometimes big, sometimes only big in my imagination. Meetings and fellowship help me keep things in perspective. Listening to others, including newcomers, reminds me that I don't know it all. Having a place to go where they welcome me, let me talk, and hug me, is a blessing. I'd be crazy to quit. I invest my time. I get paid back with interest. And the benefits continue. All I need to do is show up.

**MAY 7**

# *In This Moment, I'm doing the work.*

Recovery work is often tedious, difficult, and uncomfortable. I made a vow that I was going to successfully learn something that I wasn't good at. I attended a country western line dance class. I felt very uncomfortable at first. After a half hour of discouragement, I got up and left. Six months later I went back, determined to succeed. Again I felt awkward and uncomfortable. I had two left feet. I felt defeated by my feet. Recovery taught me to do the work. After much stumbling and persistence, I now regularly participate and even occasionally teach line dancing. It works if I work it.

**MAY 8**

# *In This Moment, I'm envious.*

I hate it when I feel envy and I was just feeling it tonight. I feel tightness in my throat and there's a knot inside my chest. I called my sponsor to talk about this flaw. Talking with her diffuses the power of the envy and I'm able to own up to it. Now, I'm entirely ready to ask God to remove this character defect.

# MAY 9

## *In This Moment,*
## *I love and accept my mother.*

I was a low priority on my mother's list. When I metaphorically said "knock, knock," I heard no response. There was no sharing of anything meaningful, no intimacy in this mother-daughter relationship. If my mother talked to anyone, it would have been her sisters.

Now, with my mother in her 80's, our relationship is evolving. My mother talks to me and even expresses feelings. I listen well, thanks to CoDA. I'm learning so much about my mother's strengths: she is emotionally stable, retains old friendships, and has developed a support system for dealing with my father's dementia.

I am grateful that I have come to know my mother better. I value our new and renewed relationship.

# MAY 10

# *In This Moment, I focus on the present.*

An important lesson I've learned in recovery is that "what if" and "if only" don't belong in my vocabulary. When the committee in my head fills me with fear and anxiety, I maintain my sanity and serenity by focusing on the present. "What if" projects to the future, which I can't control. "If only" refers to the past which I'm powerless to change. If I want healthy and loving relationships, I need to stay focused in the moment.

# MAY 11

## *In This Moment, I comfort myself.*

I was a lonely child. My parents couldn't give me the love I needed. I've been lonely ever since, desperately grasping at others to fill that void. It was very painful, until I learned new behaviors in CoDA. Now when I'm sad, lonely, or scared, I do something different. I reach within. I hug my pillow and talk to myself the way I wish my mother had talked to me. I feel comforted.

# MAY 12

## *In This Moment, I have a safety net.*

I have a favorite photo of my two-year-old grandson. He's looking at the camera with excitement and determination, while hanging in the middle of a set of monkey bars. On one side of him stands his "higher power," his dad, with hands ready to catch his beloved son should he slip. On his other side is a representative of his "fellowship" excitedly cheering him on…Grandma. I recall how it felt when I was a child, hanging from the rungs of the monkey bars, grabbing the first two bars and hanging there…scared to let go to reach for the next rung. Stuck.

I have come to believe. I have a Higher Power that stands with hands ready to catch me should I slip. I am part of a Fellowship that cheers for me. With this image in mind, I need not fear letting go.

# MAY 13

## *In This Moment, I seek balance.*

I'm aware of a need to find a balance between extremes. I want to be kind, not smothering. I want to be truthful, not brutally frank. I want to be generous, not enabling. I want to control my own behavior, not another's. I want to be an example of recovery and not lapse into the traits of codependency.

I know I can count on my Higher Power's help, today, and every day.

# MAY 14

## *In This Moment, I am whole.*

I am one with the universe. I am a complete being. I reach to connect with my Higher Power. I wish to know my soul's aspirations. I feel strength from within to heal from within. I know another human being will not complete me. My Higher Power completes me. I am whole. I am one. I am worthy of love.

# MAY 15

## *In This Moment, I let go of my ways of coping that do not work.*

When I feel tense and frustrated, if my stomach is tied up in knots, I ask myself, "Is what I am doing to cope really working? Is it making things better?" The answer is usually, "No!" I'm trying to fix the unfixable.

When my controlling and caretaking aren't working, all I need to do is let go. As the tension and frustration flow out of me, I am free to focus on the things I can control. The first thing is: What can I do to take care of myself? What do I want? More anguish or peace? The choice is obvious.

# MAY 16

## *In This Moment, my feelings become clear.*

It has taken a while, in recovery, to name and claim my feelings. It may still take me days to figure out how I feel about a particular situation. I may have to sit with that feeling until I'm able to work through it. I often discover what is true for me by writing about my feelings. It's part of my journey. As I grow and heal, my feelings become clearer, and I reap the promises of recovery.

# MAY 17

# *In This Moment, my reaction is different.*

When I was a child, I hid. I was told that "Children should be seen, but not heard." "I love you" was never spoken in my house. No one hugged. I never heard, "You did well," even though I did well in school. I didn't think I mattered much. I tried to run away at the age of ten.

Today, I know I matter. I'm not perfect, but I don't have to rely on another's approval in order to have a good self-image. I do positive self-talk. I can't change anyone else, but I can change myself and the way I treat me. When I did something weird, my first reaction was to call myself, "Stupid!" I am changing that. Today, I hit my head in the shower. My reaction was different. I said, "Oh, are you OK?"

# MAY 18

# *In This Moment, I need to take my inventory.*

I have been in CoDA for a lot of years and still experience the desire to control. I know I'm powerless over others. I know there's only one person I can control and that person is me. And to be honest, my power to control myself is limited. I need to turn over a lot of "stuff" to my Higher Power. Why do I complain and nitpick, even though I know I'm powerless? When I'm angry, when I'm critical of others, it's a signal for me to look at what I'm avoiding. I may need to set or reset a boundary. I need to look within. It's time to pray for knowledge of God's will for me. Time to go to a meeting. Time to take personal inventory and admit my wrongs. Trying to control others doesn't succeed. My CoDA program works when I work it, and I work it 'cause I'm worth it.

# MAY 19

# *In This Moment,*
# *I am free from relationship woes.*

I had been controlling, and even cajoling,

Until recovery set me free.

More aware of my feelings, I find myself healing.

I'm joyous and live happily.

Determined to stay well, my future I'll foretell.

CoDA groups are where you'll find me.

No longer perfecting, instead I'm projecting

A healthier, confident she.

Stay focused I must, in the program I trust,

And less codependent I'll be.

# MAY 20

## *In This Moment, I rejoice.*

I listen to my inner voice as it tells me what my body, mind, and spirit need. I grew up thinking the mind, body, and emotions were separate, unconnected parts. Through recovery, I learned that these parts are interconnected. What affects one part, affects all parts, whether I'm aware of these effects or not.

Today, I release the emotions I have stuffed in my body and buried in my soul. I accept my imperfections and rejoice in my humanness. As I reconnect the separated parts of me, I heal and grow. My energy increases. I hear my Higher Power's voice. I feel the love that flows through the universe. I know a new freedom.

# MAY 21

## *In This Moment, I am aware of my value and worth.*

I have finally learned that I have inherent value and worth, given to me by my Higher Power. Because I know this, I no longer need to go into a shame attack when I've made a mistake or come up short in some way. I'm now able to admit my mistakes and accept them as part of being human. I learn from my experience, as long as I stop doubting my worth or God's love for me. I have a right to be here. I am easier to live with and much more loving and accepting of my family and others. I thank God and CoDA for this knowledge.

# MAY 22

# *In This Moment, I practice.*

I learned to use affirmations in CoDA. We read them in meetings. Friends in recovery have shared their affirmation practices with me and I've learned to create my own to fit my needs. I read affirmations to myself, write them five times each, listen to my mental reactions, record and refute negatives, make signs, and post them. For more than just temporary relief, I need to believe these positive statements I'm telling myself. Recently, I had what I call "a little miracle." I made a dumb mistake but I didn't blurt out, "Stupid!" This small change was huge for me. I'm grateful to CoDA for showing me positive encouragement.

# MAY 23

## *In This Moment, I look within.*

A mirror to gaze deeply into life is a reflection of my soul.

An insatiable longing silently accompanies me.

The need for trust and love exposes me to risk.

I look within and acknowledge secrets.

Intuition guides me to fill the blank pages of my life with confidence.

Happy endings are choices to cherish.

# MAY 24

# *In This Moment,*
# *I let go of the outcome.*

I've identified a need for companionship and decided to reach out to get that need met. He may be available, he may not. I can identify my need and take action. I can't make it happen. My power doesn't go that far. I can initiate and ask to get my needs met. The outcome is up to God. Step One: I admit a need. Step Two: I accept that the fulfillment of that need is up to God. Step Three: I turn it over to God and let go of the outcome.

# MAY 25

## *In This Moment, I'm only responsible for me.*

I'm not taking responsibility for anyone else's feelings. So simple, yet this has eluded me for most of my life. The phrase "you make me feel" rang in my ears for so long — now I realize that it was manipulation. I don't accept that any more.

The feelings of others are not in my control and no one else can control mine. I am free to feel and express my feelings. I enjoy this freedom.

# MAY 26

# *In This Moment, I'm not alone.*

I have friends I can rely on who help me in my recovery.

I go to CoDA meetings to overcome the "codependent crazies."

I receive the strength to cope with my problems.

I am of service in my meeting.

I have found purpose in my life.

I overcame fear when I realized I was not alone!

# MAY 27

## *In This Moment, I'm new at this.*

CoDA? What is that?

What do you mean I'm codependent?

I don't like the sound of it!

Who's controlling whom?

Work the program?

What does that mean?

For life?

God, is this your plan to change my life for the better?

Hi, my name is _____ and I'm codependent.

# MAY 28

# *In This Moment,*
# *I listen for wisdom.*

Once it was easy and natural for me to hear my inner voice — my thoughts, feelings, and desires. When I was a little child, I knew these things intuitively and expressed them spontaneously. Then something happened to push that voice down and drown it out.

It was there all along. I hear it clearly now. When I quiet the old tapes in my mind, my inner voice comes through. It rises at the invitation as if from a long sleep. I greet my inner voice with great joy and listen for wisdom.

# MAY 29

## *In This Moment, I celebrate me.*

I never had a graduation party or celebration dinner, so recently I held my own. Just because my family of origin didn't celebrate me or my successes doesn't mean I can't acknowledge them myself. It's important for me to take the time to recognize special events or milestones in my life. That's healthy. It helps me to continue moving forward, instead of resenting "missing out" in the past. If no one else does it for me, I do it for myself. It's never too late to have a party to celebrate me!

# MAY 30

## *In This Moment, I grieve.*

Today, I am learning the importance of grief. It is a profound part of my recovery and my new life. If I deny or avoid the hurt and pain of life's losses, I deny myself. Denial of the truth may lead to my destruction. Tears of regret, remorse, and despair water the roots of love and of life itself. Failure to cry is failure to live. When I give myself the freedom to express my emotions and grieve my losses, I am comforted. Sharing with others is healing. I thank my Higher Power for guiding me along the path toward recovery.

# MAY 31

# *In This Moment, I don't have to manage everything.*

Am I trying to do it all? Am I being a perfectionist and controlling, while doing more than is appropriate? Am I feeling distress because of my behavior?

In recovery, I try healthy behavior. This is new and unfamiliar. But with repeated exercise, it becomes easier. I stop trying to manage everything and realize that I am a human being — perfectly human, not a perfect human. It's a shift in perception. With my Higher Power's guidance, unmanageability is something I can change.

# JUNE 1

## *In This Moment, my life is manageable.*

When I'm in the past, it's depression.

When I'm in the future, it's anxiety.

When I'm in the moment, it's MANAGEABLE!

# JUNE 2

## *In This Moment, I am free.*

My family does not communicate in healthy ways. I learned many family lessons growing up. Children were to be seen and not heard. Feelings were to be stuffed down. Nothing was to go outside the walls of the house. Assumptions became a way of life. I walked on eggshells, hoping to avoid saying or doing the wrong thing.

Today, I am free of those negative communication patterns. I ask directly for what I want and need and no longer make assumptions. I show respect for others by asking them what they want and need. Asking takes away the guess work. I communicate in healthy and loving ways, thanks to recovery.

# JUNE 3

## *In This Moment, I am grateful for the spiritual gifts of recovery.*

Today, I am able to tolerate a less than ideal work situation because I know I make a difference. I've acquired the patience to wait when things don't go my way. I realize the outcome is in God's hands and that I don't have to be in control. Actually, I never was. I've developed the honesty to confront the old self-righteous tapes in my head and the humility to admit my mistakes. Life's lessons are all around me. Today, I view them as opportunities for personal growth.

# JUNE 4

# *In This Moment, I'm starting a new day.*

Over the years, I've developed a morning ritual. First I ask God for a grateful heart. Then I ask that I be able to choose love over fear and anger. Since at times I am confused about what I am feeling, I ask for clarity. Next I call for help in recognizing God's plan for my life. It's easy for me to confuse my plan with my Higher Power's plan. Experience has taught me that God's plan is better. Finally I ask my Higher Power to make me useful, that I do something for somebody other than myself. Amazingly, since I've practiced this ritual, there is much less chaos in my life. Serenity is mine when I turn my life and my will over to my Higher Power.

# JUNE 5

# *In This Moment, feelings don't require action.*

I have learned in CoDA that my feelings are mostly based on early experiences, not on the present. They are important to acknowledge and reflect on, but not to act on, until I identify the source. Too often, I have acted hastily after being triggered by an issue from my family of origin. Feelings have no brains! I use my intellect in the present to choose an action. I breathe and wait. I find I have fewer regrets.

# JUNE 6

## *In This Moment, nothing changes, if nothing changes.*

I used to resist change. I found security and comfort in familiarity, even when the familiar was pain, sadness, or grief. Instead, I wanted everyone else to change so I would feel better. When I finally hit bottom, I discovered CoDA and became willing to try something different. It took time, but slowly I came to believe in the benefits of change. For me, it was the beginning of understanding that I have choices. I'm learning how to make decisions and accept responsibility for my life.

# JUNE 7

## *In This Moment, I pray for knowledge of God's will for me.*

I've come to see that my life works better when my will is in line with God's will for me. When I try to force the direction my life should take, I create resistance and problems. It's difficult. When I'm willing to work Step Eleven on a daily basis, I find my life goes more smoothly. I pray for knowledge of God's will for me and the power to carry it out. It's that simple!

# JUNE 8

# *In This Moment, I set a goal.*

It's a tradition! Every year since I've been in CoDA, I set a new goal for myself. Once it was for balance, because I tend to do black and white thinking. Another year it was to be more forgiving. I did some intense forgiveness work that year, forgiving the young man who raped and beat my granddaughter. I didn't do it for him. I did it for me. The anger was eating me alive.

This year my goal is acceptance of life on life's terms. I meet my goal when I remember to surrender. I ask for help to know God's will for me and for the power to carry it out.

# JUNE 9

# *In This Moment,*
# *I follow the rules.*

Years ago, I scribbled three things on the inside cover of my CoDA book. The Golden Rule, which is "Do unto others as you would have them do unto you;" the Silver Rule, which is "Do unto yourself what you would do for others," and the Iron Rule, which is "Don't do for others what they can do for themselves."

As a codependent, I tend to either attempt to dominate others or find myself overly dependent on them. I need to make a conscious effort to follow these rules in my recovery, until they become second nature.

# JUNE 10

## *In This Moment, I feel free.*

In my codependence, I've had trouble making decisions, even small ones. I'm getting better at it now. One of the best decisions I made was joining a CoDA group a couple of years ago, and attending regularly. I know now that I have a right to make decisions and have my own opinions. I'm pleased with most of the decisions I make and consider all my choices to be learning experiences. I feel free and I want to stay that way.

# JUNE 11

## *In This Moment, I'm glad I'm in recovery.*

I'm looking at codependent behaviors (mine) and trying to change them one day at a time. I'm not ashamed to be codependent. Being in CoDA is helping me. I have the Twelve Steps to guide me. I have found good friends in meetings and I'm learning how to have healthy relationships. I'm finding the courage to ask for what I need and to say, "No." I take an active part in meeting my own needs, instead of being resentful when others don't do it for me. Recovery work has changed my life for the better.

# JUNE 12

# *In This Moment,*
# *I thank my*
# *Higher Power for gifts.*

Before CoDA, I could not make myself heard. Nobody listened to me. Since I joined CoDA, that has changed. My family and friends listen. Before CoDA, I resented my parents. I wanted to replace my childhood with a happier one. In recovery, I discovered my powerlessness over others and my past. I came to accept my parents as imperfect humans who tried their best. Before CoDA, it was hard to leave my house. Learning about and attending CoDA meetings expanded my world. Before CoDA, I felt "less than" just about everybody. Now my relationships are with equals. Before CoDA, I wondered if I could ever love someone. Now I know I am capable of a deep love for another. I am so grateful for these gifts. Thank you, Higher Power. Thank you, CoDA.

# JUNE 13

# *In This Moment, I am at peace.*

What a joy to be living God's will and not mine. When I forget how important it is to spend some quiet time each day with myself and my Higher Power, I find my life becoming unmanageable and my addictions call out to me. I love Third Step work because of the peace I experience. I remember everything is in God's hands. I trust the outcome and I don't have to fight the things over which I am powerless. My codependency is a difficult thing to outgrow, but with God's help, I am making a lot of progress. I use the Steps to get my thinking sorted out and stay on track.

# JUNE 14

# *In This Moment, shall we hug?*

I'm not always comfortable hugging in CoDA. If someone asks if I want a hug, I'm codependently reluctant to refuse. With practice, though, I'm learning to say, "no."

But what if the person doesn't ask first? The *Newcomers Handbook* recommends that we decline a hug "in a non-shaming way." What is a non-shaming way to back off from an unwelcome attempt to hug me? Is "I don't want a hug" firm enough for someone who is violating my space and my body? Is "STOP IT" shaming?

I want to protect myself with appropriate boundaries. I'm searching for how I can "say what I mean and mean what I say, in a non-shaming way."

# JUNE 15

## *In This Moment, I'm in the moment.*

I just remembered a past event that brought up some strong feelings. I examine how I felt then. I feel my feelings again. I trust that I am being healed. I release my fear. I have the option to look at my choices. I make my decision to act or wait. I'm at peace.

# JUNE 16

# *In This Moment,*
# *I receive my answer.*

I had a very serious decision to make regarding my future. In bed at 6 a.m., I prayed to the God of my understanding, "Please help me make the right decision. Show me a sign." Immediately, words and phrases began racing through my mind. The answer became very clear, very quickly. I knew from prior experiences to get out of bed, grab a pencil and paper, and write down my thoughts. I thanked God and looked at the clock. It was 6:16 — my birthdate. What a gift! Peace of mind, clarity of thought, and knowing beyond a doubt that God is nearby.

# JUNE 17

# *In This Moment, I do what I need to do.*

I don't have to have everything figured out because it's not all up to me. All I have to do is take the next step of faith. It may be time to walk into a courtroom. It may be time to initiate a talk with a friend about a disagreement. It may be time to pay my bills. It may be time to say no. It may be time to say yes. It may be time to let go. Faith in my Higher Power means I trust that all is well. I take the next step, even if I'm shaking.

# JUNE 18

# *In This Moment, grant me strength.*

Grant me strength to trust in this day. To believe that being me — and all that means — is OK. Give me strength to breathe through the difficult moments I face. Give me hope that they will pass. Help me smile and even laugh. Help me trust that my body, my words, and my energy are all that is needed. Give me the confidence to believe that my decisions are the best I can make.

Today, I choose to see beauty. I'm grateful for whatever God sends my way.

# JUNE 19

## *In This Moment, I feel renewed.*

Each day is a celebration.

The need to find meaning is satisfied.

I cherish myself above all.

I am joyous and peaceful.

I recognize the presence, power, and light of my soul.

My Higher Power calms and renews my spirit.

# JUNE 20

# *In This Moment,*
# *I accept imperfection.*

The Steps remind me to practice CoDA principles in all my affairs. They don't tell me to be perfect. Once I was my own worst enemy. Trying to be perfect was a self-defeating prophecy. The committee in my head did not hold meetings in my favor. I lived my life filled with shame-based fear.

Thanks to the Steps, I am aware of my shortcomings. I'm not perfect. Today, I am perfectly fine being an imperfect human being.

By practicing self-care, I find acceptance of who I am. Healthy, respectful communication starts with me. I celebrate my successes, growth, and accomplishments with gratitude.

# JUNE 21

## *In This Moment, I see situations and people as they truly are.*

I see my present clearly, instead of allowing the clouds of the past to obscure it. I no longer project my past or parents onto situations or people. I react to the situation to the degree that it warrants. Because I have compassion for myself, I now have greater compassion for others. I see the hurt child behind my own unhealthy behaviors, as well as the hurtful behaviors of others. Hurt people hurt people. Healthy people are loving to others. I am becoming a healthy person.

# JUNE 22

## *In This Moment, I trust those who are trustworthy.*

In my CoDA group, I find people who understand me in a way few others can. I trust them with information about me that I cannot easily share with others. I trust that my CoDA friends won't judge me, criticize me, tell me not to feel that way, or try to fix me. I have learned to trust selectively and wisely.

# JUNE 23

# *In This Moment, I'm co-sponsoring.*

My co-sponsor and I have a great relationship, in spite of the fact that we live thousands of miles apart. We communicate through e-mail. We are working from CoDA's *The Twelve Steps & Twelve Traditions Workbook*. We answer the questions and share with one another. We did an electronic Fifth Step. I'm working my recovery program on a deeper level. As a result, I'm learning more about myself.

# JUNE 24

## *In This Moment, I practice self-care.*

I'm exhausted. So much of my energy has been spent helping others that I have too little left over to do what's important to me. I do for others what I would be better off doing for myself. CoDA has led me to understand that I need to focus on myself first. This does not mean that others, whom I love, will suffer. They'll still love me. It means that I am better able to look after myself. Only then can I interact with my family with energy and enthusiasm.

# JUNE 25

# *In This Moment, I'm grateful for the bad times.*

I'm grateful for all my life experiences, good and bad. If I could go back in time, do things differently, and have only "good" days, who would I be? I know I wouldn't be who I am today. The good days are smooth sailing and fun, but I've learned so much about myself from those bad days. The bad times test my strength and open my eyes to the issues I need to address. I now see painful experiences as growth opportunities. At these times, I travel further along the road of recovery.

# JUNE 26

# *In This Moment, I am taking a test.*

I am newly married, after five years of widowhood and active CoDA membership. My goal now is to draw a line between being too compliant and making unnecessary trouble. My new husband is a retired military man. He believes in equal participation in marriage — or so he says. But his professional experience makes his automatic responses a bit autocratic. My experience makes my first reaction, "Yes, dear" and I go along to get along. We are both working to achieve a balance in this marriage. I consider this process to be my final exam in CoDA. I know I will never graduate, but I want to experience progress rather than perfection.

# JUNE 27

# *In This Moment, I focus on the lesson.*

Instead of getting frustrated that the same situation is happening again and again, I try to discover the lesson that I need to learn. My Higher Power continues to put people and situations in my path that encourage me to grow. These painful experiences continue until I change my behavior, my attitude, or both. I have faith that my Higher Power supports me and wants me to be happy. I trust that things will work out.

# JUNE 28

# *In This Moment, I choose not to absorb negativity.*

I used to feel like a psychic sponge, just soaking up whatever feelings were around me — a codependent chameleon. Through working my program, I am solidifying my boundaries. I know what is acceptable and unacceptable behavior for me. No one has the authority to determine this for me, but me. I am my own sovereign. In this moment, I simply observe, not absorb, someone else's feelings. I monitor my thoughts and gently shift them away when negativity arises. I do not engage in gossip. I focus on me.

# JUNE 29

## *In This Moment, I strive for rigorous honesty.*

I'm not perfect. I can't be rigorously honest all of the time, but I can strive toward that goal. When I fall short, I work the Tenth Step to get myself back on track. As I become honest about my actions, I also become accountable for those actions and any pain they may have caused. I think long and hard about the consequences of my actions and find I'm less likely to do things I wouldn't want others to know about. When I strive to be rigorously honest, I travel further along the road of recovery.

# JUNE 30

# *In This Moment, I allow myself rest.*

Why is it so hard for me to recognize that I need rest? Rest is part of the natural cycle for all living things. When I'm overworked, overextended, or my emotions are raw, I deserve a break. For me, relaxing doesn't mean taking a long nap. It means doing those things that calm and soothe my soul, as well as my mind and body. Relaxing helps recharge me so that I'm more enthusiastic and effective. Resting when I need it is not selfish. It is self-loving.

# JULY 1

## *In This Moment, I experience joy.*

Sometimes I was afraid to be happy — afraid that I would experience a little bliss and something or someone would snatch it away. As a child, this happened many times and reinforced those beliefs. I am now an adult. I make choices; I create my own happiness and joy. No one can take it from me unless I let them. I choose to bring into my life situations and people that bring me joy. I give myself permission to feel absolutely wonderful.

# JULY 2

## *In This Moment, I overcome my fears.*

Most of the time I didn't know what I wanted, what I felt, or even what I needed. I used to fear change. Then I came to CoDA. Now, I realize that change is necessary for my growth. I have choices and take responsibility for my decisions. I love and accept myself and others. I have healthy relationships. I acknowledge my feelings and deal with my issues. I have the courage to change the things I can. "I am no longer controlled by my fears. I overcome my fears and act with courage, integrity, and dignity." (Second Promise.)

# JULY 3

## *In This Moment, I wonder what happened.*

What happened to the man I loved? Does he still love books and music? Is he as charming as ever? Does he carry me somewhere in his heart, the way I do him? In this relationship, I felt alive and joyful. But it wasn't meant to last — our individual lives took us elsewhere. The end was painful, filled with grief and tears.

Today, I thank my Higher Power for the experience: the joy I felt, the support I got when it ended, the strength to endure the shocking pain, and the hope to mend and go on.

# JULY 4

## *In This Moment, I am independent of the opinion of others.*

I was raised in a family where "What will the neighbors think?" was the most important consideration for my parents. I find it's not easy to overcome my childhood programming, but I'm working toward that goal. I know I can't please everyone, nor should I try. As long as I'm not engaging in harmful behaviors, what I do is no one else's business. I live my life in a way that makes me happy, regardless of what others think.

# JULY 5

## *In This Moment, I accept change.*

I don't like change! For me, it's equivalent to surrender, something I don't want to do. When I finally receive the willingness to surrender, I feel free. Is it the rebellious child within, or my adult rigidity, that keeps me stuck in the problem? When I remember that acceptance is the answer, I move faster into surrender. I realize the only things over which I have any control are what I think and what I do. Daily prayers for the "knowledge of God's will . . . and the power to carry that out" help me realize that the only certainty in life is change. Why would I want to clutter my day with resistance? When I am open-minded, ready to listen, and willing to go to any lengths, the solution appears.

# JULY 6

## *In This Moment, my relationships are real.*

A certain sense of hero worship while growing up may be understandable, but I saw nothing wrong with making other people, such as parents, teachers, or bosses, my Gods. I thought if I worked hard enough and accomplished enough, they'd have to love me, or at least respect me. External validation was never enough. Disillusionment ultimately set in because these authority figures were only human.

Today, as I work my CoDA program, I have a true Higher Power. Although it has taken me many years to understand this aspect of my codependency, it is worth the journey. My relationship with my Higher Power allows me to have realistic relationships with other human beings.

# JULY 7

# *In This Moment, my search for love is over.*

My Higher Power loves me unconditionally. My family loves me to the best of their ability. My friends give and receive love in an unending circle. I am blessed. While I long for a primary relationship, I know it will happen when I am ready. Then I will be free to love a partner without fear of loss, because I can't lose the love I already have. When I enter into a relationship without fear and insecurity, I am free to be my lovable self.

# JULY 8

## *In This Moment, a door opens.*

My office has just been closed. I'm not eligible to collect unemployment insurance because I got this job with a temp agency eleven months ago. I am now an expert on a particular computer program that will no longer be used in this area. I could be bitter, but my bosses and co-workers have enriched me. I have learned a lot. Also, I was able to save a bit of money which will keep me going for awhile. I'm looking forward to some time off, to think, to grow, and to write. I'm grateful that I can afford time off for awhile. What I first saw as an injustice has become a blessing.

# JULY 9

# *In This Moment, I'm not in charge.*

Thank you, Higher Power, for my family, my friends, my home, my pets, my health, my job, enough money to pay my bills, help to quit smoking, and a healthy grandchild. I'm not in a love relationship today and I can honestly say, "Thank you for my freedom!" I have so much to be grateful for. My life is pretty good. I used to envy people who seemed to have more than I did and I felt unhappy. I used to manipulate and control others. I wound up feeling frustrated and resentful. I don't do that anymore.

Today, I let go of the need to control. I'm not in charge! What a relief!

# JULY 10

## *In This Moment, I walk the walk.*

No matter how hard the journey, there is always a principle in the CoDA program that answers my need. I remember many frightening times filled with questions, yet knowing that the answers would come. I put my trust in the program. I walk toward what I perceive as wellness. And sure enough, when I get to the other side, the lesson becomes clear. I am grateful for the many ways the principles of recovery are woven into my life.

# JULY 11

## *In This Moment, I am breaking a habit.*

I have been a smoker for 42 years. Last week, I saw a journalist on TV announce that he has lung cancer. I knew it was time for me to quit. I heard that when you quit an addiction, a lot of feelings start coming out. I've recently gone back to daily journaling. Hopefully, this tool will help me deal with my emotions. My friends in the program encourage and support me. With my Higher Power's help, I'll kick it, one day at a time.

# JULY 12

## *In This Moment, I remember that codependence sells, but I don't have to buy.*

When I first came into CoDA, I began to realize how many popular songs are filled with codependent lyrics. Apparently, there are big bucks to be made being codependent and singing about it. Recognizing this created a dilemma for me. At first I wanted to stop listening to any songs with codependent lyrics, thinking they might keep me stuck in codependent ways. Soon I found my selections very limited.

As I grew and healed, I found that I could still enjoy some of my favorite codependent songs, for the beauty of the singer's voice, the music, or just the pleasant reminder that I've overcome such behaviors in my life.

# JULY 13

# *In This Moment, I live in the present.*

I often find my mind wandering back in time, replaying past situations in a distorted manner. I am bombarded with negative thoughts like "If only I could have made that person like me, I wouldn't be alone today," or "I shouldn't have reacted that way," or "Why do the same things keep happening to me over and over?" or "That person really wasn't so bad, maybe it was just me," or "If I were prettier, funnier, smarter, that person wouldn't have left me," and the clincher, "It was all my fault." When these thoughts start whirling around in my head, the best thing for me to do is turn my life over to the care of God. I release worry, guilt, and regret about my past. I ask for the strength and guidance needed to change my old ways of thinking, feeling, and reacting. Slowly, but surely, I realize that there is no future in the past.

# JULY 14

## *In This Moment, I go alone.*

It's not that I prefer to be alone, or don't want a companion who enjoys the things I like, but I don't let the absence of a friend keep me from doing the things I want to do. I no longer stay home and feel sorry for myself, or go where others want to go, even though I don't. Sometimes, I travel to new places. Sometimes, I sit on the beach alone. I'm working to be true to myself. If a healthy relationship is in my future, I'm ready.

# JULY 15

## *In This Moment, I am no longer chained.*

I came to CoDA because I was desperate. My family was driving me crazy with their demands. In CoDA, I learned about setting boundaries. I just said, "No." I stopped doing for them what they could do for themselves. At first, my family didn't like the changes in me. After a while, they realized I wasn't going to go back to caretaking them. When I take care of myself and do what makes me happy, my spirit and my life improve. I no longer feel chained to my family. I am so grateful for CoDA meetings and the people there.

# JULY 16

# *In This Moment, I choose to wait.*

I'm working Step Three. I feel an urgent need to DO SOMETHING, but the way is not clear. I have no sense of peace. Doing nothing in these situations, choosing to wait instead of acting in panic and urgency, is an act of faith. I wait and turn the problem and solution over to my Higher Power. It may seem irresponsible or lazy, but I choose to see it positively and call it letting go. When the time comes, I will act.

For now, I am doing nothing except "turning it over" to my Higher Power. That is doing something powerful. That is faith.

# JULY 17

## *In This Moment, I am patient with my own recovery.*

I am unique, with my own history, feelings, and life experiences. I must build a strong foundation with myself first and that takes time. I take one step at a time, working my recovery completely and thoroughly. Otherwise, it would be as if I were painting the walls on a house whose foundation is collapsing. There is no need to rush. I am on God's time and schedule. Everything is unfolding as it should and the pattern will be beautiful.

# JULY 18

## *In This Moment,*
## *I put myself first.*

Whenever I put myself on hold, my life goes haywire. Putting myself first doesn't mean that I neglect those I care about. It means that I don't neglect myself. If I neglect myself, I'm not helping anyone.

When I put myself first in my own life, when I take responsibility for meeting my own needs, then I can be available for those I care about in a healthy way. It doesn't come naturally yet. I have to make a conscious effort. Today, I choose to put myself first when I make decisions.

# JULY 19

# *In This Moment,*
# *I'm glad I have a sponsor.*

I've had many sponsors over the years. Some lasted for a day, a week, a month, or a year. They all helped me along on my journey. They taught me stuff I didn't even know I needed to learn. My current sponsor listens when I need to vent. She shares her experience, strength, and hope with me. She doesn't "should" on me. She doesn't tell me I'm crazy. She accepts me. The relationship I have with my sponsor is very special.

# JULY 20

## *In This Moment, feelings are my guide.*

For years, I denied my feelings and pretended that things were OK. I allowed others to treat me in inappropriate ways. Then I arrived at a point in recovery where my feelings became too strong to ignore. I finally blew. I was surprised by the depth of emotion that had been buried for so many years.

In CoDA, I'm working on my issues and feelings are my guide along the path of recovery. I don't have to act on them. As I surrender to them, I learn from the wisdom they offer.

# JULY 21

# *In This Moment,*
# *I'm in the right place.*

On a hot, steamy day in July, I walked to my first CoDA meeting. I was lonely and feeling a lot of pain. After getting a wrong address and walking six extra blocks, I finally found the building. The sign outside read, "This is the place." And it was the place where I found acceptance, safety, healthy behavior, friends, recovery, and hope.

Looking back, I believe my Higher Power led me there. Because I am a bit of a skeptic, my Higher Power provided the sign to assure me that I was where I needed to be. I didn't know about the Third Step that first day, but I was able to acknowledge my pain, and trust that I would find help in recovery.

# JULY 22

## *In This Moment, I seek interdependence.*

I've had my share of broken relationships. Not until I began attending CoDA was I able to see my part in the breakups. Today, I have a relationship with a person who is very different from me. When we argue, I mentally review our incompatibilities. Then, I compare our shared values: a belief in God, family loyalty, honesty, trust, and dependability. I admit I enjoy our time spent together: dancing, camping, movies, the beach, our kitty, yard sales, and traveling. I like the "give and take," "teach and learn," aspects of our relationship. We are partners with a common goal of making this relationship work. In this moment, I am interdependent.

# JULY 23

## *In This Moment, I savor my senses.*

My feelings are real. They are the result of all that my senses report to my brain, based not just in the moment, but also on my history. In the past, I could see and hear, but did not appreciate the way my brain brought all the inputs together. My feelings and reactions build upon all of the information that my senses report. I am aware of my senses and have learned to value them. It is through them that I identify my feelings. I like this journey of self-discovery.

# JULY 24

## *In This Moment,*
## *I am a recovering codependent.*

I clearly see how I learned to be codependent in my childhood. I was shamed, neglected, invalidated, and forced to take on responsibilities too heavy for my age. Sometimes, people praised and complimented me for my codependent behavior! They couldn't see that my "unselfish" behavior was damaging.

Now, I am learning healthy new behaviors, communication skills, and ways to respond. I practice my skills by interacting with other recovering codependents. I get support and encouragement from the Fellowship.

# JULY 25

## *In This Moment, I feel safe.*

As a youngster, I was not allowed to cry, speak, or scream. I carried the burden of my parents' truth. My childhood was not happy; it wasn't a safe place to be. I was alone. I didn't question. For years I kept the family secrets. I looked just fine on the outside, but inside I was a mess.

Many years later, I found a safe place in CoDA meetings. I discovered people I could trust. I saw my parents' characteristics in others and their truth helped set me free. I found brothers and sisters at every meeting. In CoDA, I found my true family and my authentic self.

# JULY 26

## *In This Moment, I know a new freedom.*

I shared about my sister at a meeting recently and realized if I didn't let go of that issue, God couldn't take it. Deep inside, I had been feeling responsible for my sister, thinking I was the one to "fix" her. I've come to understand the arrogance of that belief. My Higher Power wants me to let go of things that aren't mine. When I remember this, I feel lighter. One of the CoDA Promises has come true…"I know a new freedom."

# JULY 27

## *In This Moment, I see the good part of my character.*

It's so easy to find fault with myself. My parents did it first. Then I did it to myself for years. I'm changing. My Fourth Step helped me to stop making "all or nothing" judgments of my character. I'm not perfect, but I'm not all bad either. I look for, and acknowledge, my good qualities which I honor in my moral inventory. It helps to balance the scale and create a more realistic picture of myself.

# JULY 28

# *In This Moment, I'm humble.*

Before I make amends, I check with my Higher Power in prayer. If I have confusion or doubt — which is most of the time — I check with my sponsor, who shares experience, strength, and hope. It's humbling to acknowledge that I'm not perfect, that I have erred. It takes me out of my self-centeredness to recognize that my actions may have hurt another.

Making amends isn't about the outcome or how the other person reacts. It's about changing my behavior. Change is tough, but it's necessary to my recovery.

# JULY 29

## *In This Moment, I forgive.*

I forgive myself for hurting others. I forgive others for hurting me. Forgiveness does not mean that I sanction the abuse or pain. It just means that I give the situation over to my Higher Power, so that I may be free from the resentments, anger, and pain that keep me from fully experiencing my present. I may or may not choose to tell someone that I have forgiven them, or do anything about it. If I am holding on to guilt because of something I did, I make appropriate amends. I no longer feel shame for who I am. I am whole. I am lovable.

# JULY 30

## *In This Moment, I'm changing my behavior.*

When I make amends, not only do I apologize for the harm I've caused in the past, but I also commit to change my behavior in the future. Although the other person may benefit, it's not about the other person; it's about my own peace of mind and spirit. Walking through a difficult amends cleanses my soul. In making amends, I become spiritually whole.

# JULY 31

## *In This Moment, I feel my feelings.*

My feelings do not define me. They are neither good nor bad — they just are. How long I hold onto my feelings, especially resentments, is my choice. If I feel overwhelmed by my feelings, I take a time out. I respect the place where I am. I acknowledge my feelings. They won't go away simply because I ignore or deny them. I need to share them with someone I trust. I find an environment where I feel safe, such as a CoDA meeting, where I can express a full range of emotions. It's such a relief not to worry about being judged or criticized.

I now know what my feelings are and I express them in healthy ways. Thank you, CoDA!

# AUGUST 1

# *In This Moment,*
# *I choose who I am.*

I've decided to become the person I want to be — physically, emotionally, intellectually, and spiritually. I consciously focus on specific growth areas, letting go of those negative traits and character defects that hold me back. Working the Fourth and Fifth Steps helps me identify who I am and who I want to be. The Tenth Step helps keep me on track. I am no longer defined or controlled by anyone else. I claim my right to be who I really am.

# AUGUST 2

## *In This Moment, I live the Steps.*

I am dedicated to living the Twelve Steps every day of my life. As I recognize and own my flaws, I appreciate the gifts I have received through working my CoDA program. I thank God daily for my spirituality and wisdom. I give back through service work what has so generously been provided to me. It's not necessarily what I know that helps me grow, but, rather, how I apply what I know.

# AUGUST 3

## *In This Moment, I'm open to trying what works for others.*

My sponsor shared that he gets on his knees every morning and prays. He shared that it immediately made a dramatic change in how his life was going. I knew I should follow his example, but at first I wanted nothing to do with getting on my knees. Becoming subservient to anyone or anything was not on my "to do" list. But I humbled myself and began getting on my knees every morning just to see what would happen. Now, I know that I had been trying to run the show. I didn't fully trust my Higher Power. I was so surprised when the same thing happened to me. My life began to change.

# AUGUST 4

## *In This Moment,*
## *I'm comfortable with myself.*

Now I know what I am. I'm codependent. And I have good news — I have a CoDA home group. One day at a time, I react differently. My self-talk is more positive. I'm beginning to like myself as I am. Some people may not like me and that's OK now. If the cost of their approval is to deny my true self, the price is too high. Every day I work my recovery, and with God's guidance, I'm making changes.

# AUGUST 5

# *In This Moment, I affirm myself.*

I came into CoDA at a time when my life was pretty chaotic. I felt worthless and ashamed about my childhood. CoDA meetings helped me put most of that shame to rest. Affirmations help me feel better about myself as I take life one day at a time. Before CoDA, when a friend or family member had a problem, my first reaction was wanting to fix it. Today, I know what's my business and what's not. I learned in CoDA that I'm powerless over others. That's a good thing for me to remember.

# AUGUST 6

# *In This Moment,*
# *I am more honest.*

When I arrived in CoDA five years ago, I was sick and tired of trying to control what others thought of me. I remember, as a child, trying so hard to impress others so that I would be accepted. As an adult, I pretended to be whatever I thought would make others like me.

In CoDA, taking a good look at myself, I see that dishonesty never helped me. I am honest when I share in meetings and people there accept me. I am trying to live a healthier life with the help of the Twelve Steps and Twelve Traditions of CoDA.

# AUGUST 7

# *In This Moment,*
# *I feel more sane.*

I need not worry about fixing myself, nor take on the "codependent crazies" alone. I need not be overwhelmed by the complexities of life. Surely, relief and healing are around the corner. Step Two teaches me to believe that a power greater than myself can restore me to sanity. I've seen many signs that demonstrate to me, over and over, that my Higher Power loves me unconditionally. All I need to do is surrender to that positive spiritual force.

# AUGUST 8

## *In This Moment, I consider the view.*

When my recovery family went camping, I got a lesson in perspective. The second morning, upon awakening, I looked out the triangular crack between the door and rain cover. I saw red. That's all I saw. No matter how I turned to look out my "window," all I saw was red. It really puzzled me, because the day before I hadn't noticed much of anything red.

What a difference in perspective when I went outside. The red that had been so dominant from my bedside was a red cooler. In the larger picture, the cooler was but a small part of the picture.

Now, I understand how the wrong perspective has hindered my recovery. How often I allow small things to loom large. Recovery gives me a bigger picture. When I'm stuck, I look at my situation from another perspective. My world is a much friendlier place.

# AUGUST 9

# *In This Moment, I let go.*

I just read the cancellation notice regarding my homeowner's insurance. I fear a world of red tape will have to be conquered to fix this. I have no time. I have no energy. I start to panic, then realize: I can let go. I do Steps One, Two, and Three. I put the envelope down and find a quiet spot to pray. I tell God this is more than I can handle. It comes to me; I have the answer I need. I say: "I'm turning this over to you. Show me what the next step is; I trust you."

# **AUGUST 10**

# *In This Moment,*
# *I trust in my Higher Power.*

I do not worry about the future or regret the past. The same power that causes the sun to rise each morning and provides light and sustenance to the earth can handle my issues, no matter how small or large. I am but one creation in this vast sea of creation, yet my part is vital.

As I am someone's student, so I am also another's teacher. My Higher Power has created me and placed me here. Although I may not always understand my purpose, I belong here simply because I am.

# AUGUST 11

## *In This Moment, I let go of what others think about me.*

When I seek attention and praise, or fear ridicule and rejection, my connection to God is weakened. I find myself treating others as if they were my God. Turning to my Higher Power for help, attention, and love frees me from codependent behaviors. Trusting a power greater than myself allows me to feel peaceful and secure. I know that God will provide the guidance I need.

# AUGUST 12

# *In This Moment, I stop blaming myself.*

In the past, I made poor choices in relationships. This habit stems from a childhood of emotional neglect and abandonment. As a result of these poor choices, I have a string of failed friendships. I often shouldered the burden for these failures. I believed that others valued me only for my deeds or my ability to "fix" their problems.

Now, in recovery, I've come to believe that a relationship is far from a failure when it teaches me something. I no longer blame myself when a relationship ends.

# AUGUST 13

## *In This Moment, I choose not to listen to my disease.*

Even though I work the CoDA program, sometimes the demons in my mind pick the locks on their cages. They run around knocking over the furniture, scattering the mail, and teasing the cat. Chaos reigns and I feel insane. I have learned that when the demons of my codependency speak, I can choose not to listen. My codependency tells me that I have no value, I'll never get it right, and I would be better off dead.

In recovery, I know those things are not true and so it must be my disease talking. My disease causes me to suffer and feel insane. My Higher Power restores me to sanity. As I rely on my Higher Power for guidance, my codependency loses its power. I am precious and free.

# AUGUST 14

## *In This Moment, I love my muscles.*

When I was new in recovery, I hated a lot of things about myself, including my (flabby) body.

After going to CoDA meetings for a while, I "came to believe" that regular exercise was one way to take care of myself. When I started working out, I felt self-conscious and awkward.

Since I've been exercising several times a week, I'm developing muscles. I love feeling stronger.

# AUGUST 15

# *In This Moment,*
# *I feel satisfied with my life.*

It's the middle of the week. I'm leaving for vacation tomorrow. Somehow, I managed to complete all the week's work tasks by the end of the day today. It's amazing how, if I put my mind to it, I can be very focused and productive. Being in CoDA helps me to concentrate on those things I need to do, rather than looking around for people who require my "help." Working the Steps, especially Step Three, allows me to cease worrying about things that aren't my business. I don't have to be in control. I just have to show up. My Higher Power leads the way.

# AUGUST 16

# *In This Moment, I'm healing.*

A few months ago, I developed a panic disorder when I remembered my childhood fear of getting polio. When polio was at its height, I was taking care of my younger brother and sister while my mother worked. I was terrified of getting sick, but I had to be brave and keep things together for my mother's sake. I was ten years old.

In CoDA, I am healing from my painful childhood. I am learning to re-parent the little one who had to grow up too fast. I turn to the God of my understanding and ask for healing.

# AUGUST 17

# *In This Moment,*
# *I feel and express joy.*

Spending time getting to know my grandchildren, and letting them get to know me, brings me so much joy. Through their eyes I see that the world is filled with simple pleasures. As a child, I felt that freedom, but as I grew up, I thought I had to act as a responsible adult. When my children were growing up, I took life more seriously and missed out on many good times with them. Recovery in CoDA has helped me get back in touch with my inner child. Today, I can feel and express joy.

# AUGUST 18

# *In This Moment, I'm grateful for the opportunity to grow.*

My boss, with whom I'd had difficulties, moved on to another job. I was so relieved. A temporary director from another facility came to manage the program. The staff flourished under her strict, but consistently fair rule. Four months later, my ex boss reapplied and was hired. When I heard, I recited the *Serenity Prayer* over and over. This situation was one of those things "I cannot change." I wasn't willing to abandon my job, so I needed to change my attitude. When I became more open-minded, I saw that my boss had changed as well; he was more patient and a better communicator. Life in recovery is full of surprises and opportunities for growth.

# AUGUST 19

# *In This Moment,*
# *I allow myself to be imperfect.*

When I don't feel good enough and I start thinking of all I've "done wrong" — or what's "gone wrong" — in my life, I close my eyes and breathe for a minute. I think about the beautiful things in my world: trees, skies, animals, and water. This universe has amazing organization and structure, but it's not perfect. With recovery, I give myself permission to have the same standards. Affirming that I am "good enough" helps me stop judging myself. I go forward today without regret.

# AUGUST 20

# *In This Moment, I am loved.*

I put my life into my Higher Power's hands and trust that I am loved. My recovery life is an adventure, complete with challenges, opportunities, and oh-so-wonderful surprises! I can be my own best friend!

I've learned to give my love to one who really needs it — me.

# AUGUST 21

# *In This Moment,*
# *I am aware.*

The Twelve Promises of CoDA sound too good to be true. But they are promises, not possibilities. One at a time, they seem to be coming true for me. Right now, I'm especially grateful for the fourth one, "I release myself from worry, guilt, and regret about my past and present. I am aware enough not to repeat it." This is about forgiveness. I've forgiven myself for mistakes of the past, but I'm not yet aware enough to completely avoid the old bad habits. Sometimes, recovery seems to be two steps forward, one step back. This Promise assures me that the more aware I become, the better my life will be.

# AUGUST 22

## *In This Moment, I recognize each person's individuality.*

We are all different. My reactions and feelings are based upon the experiences of my life, starting with a childhood that I do not fully recall. My reactions and feelings are not the same as those of others in similar situations. I have learned that I cannot expect others to respond or act in the same way I do in a given situation. They are who they are. I am who I am.

# AUGUST 23

# *In This Moment,*
# *I choose the path of recovery.*

My Higher Power has given me the gift of free will. I choose recovery and ask for guidance. With God's help, I release harmful negativity. I envision myself protected and loved. Love and positive energy surround me. The program of Co-Dependents Anonymous is my chosen path.

# AUGUST 24

## *In This Moment,*
## *I toss my medallion in the air.*

Sometimes, I need to make a decision and just can't decide what to do. So I get out my CoDA anniversary medallion. Then, I flip the medallion in the air, instead of a coin. Flipping that CoDA medallion reminds me that my Higher Power is in control. It reminds me that I'm powerless over the outcome, no matter what I decide. It reminds me that decisions can be revisited if need be. It reminds me to let go and turn my life over to my Higher Power, yet again. Every time I toss my medallion, I am reminded of how far I have come on my journey.

# AUGUST 25

## *In This Moment, I value service.*

When my marriage ended, I had more time on my hands than I knew what to do with. My social circle was nil, because my friends had all been wives of my husband's friends and were no longer willing to be in my life. Service in CoDA filled a void. Over time, I came to appreciate the benefits of service work: meeting new people, feeling good while making others feel welcome, having more self-confidence, and even some travel. Service work has enriched my life.

# AUGUST 26

## *In This Moment, I accept powerlessness.*

Once I embraced the concept of powerlessness over other people, places, and things, I was faced with learning to accept "the things I cannot change." I questioned what it meant to accept something, even when chaos surrounded me. It dawned on me — I don't have to like what's going on nor do I have to agree with it. I only need to stop trying to change the person or the situation. I've learned to let go and, as a result, I feel inner peace.

# AUGUST 27

## *In This Moment, I like freedom.*

After my husband's death, I felt stressed if I made a decision that he might not have approved. Even something small. Would he like those new curtains? I lacked confidence and felt insignificant. Then I found CoDA. Now, I have purpose in my life — taking care of me! I make my own decisions and I'm pleased with most of them. Someday, I may have another man in my life. Thanks to CoDA, I won't give away my right to have opinions and make decisions. I'm free and I like it.

# AUGUST 28

# *In This Moment, I face the day.*

Too often, I awoke in the morning still tired and headachy after a fitful night of tossing and turning. I'd head for the medicine cabinet to take some aspirin. Now, I'm aware I was treating the symptoms, not the cause. I had been going to bed still worried about things I could not control. I would wake up in the night and have trouble falling back to sleep, because I was trying to solve other people's problems.

In CoDA, I have learned to "let it go." I sleep better and wake refreshed. I'm ready to face the coming day.

# AUGUST 29

# *In This Moment, I surrender.*

I am no longer a victim. I take responsibility for myself. I surrender, because I am making a conscious choice to do so. Surrender is not an act of weakness, but one of strength and choice. I choose to surrender to allow a new way of living to enter my life and being. My Higher Power's wisdom is vast and encompasses so much more than I could ever individually know. I trust that through whatever comes, the result will be the greatest good for all. Surrender is the beginning of freedom.

# AUGUST 30

# *In This Moment, I deserve it.*

In my first marriage, before recovery, I was so immersed in the bad times — resenting them, predicting them, and complaining about them — that I wasn't able to enjoy the good times. Then I started going to CoDA meetings and spent a number of years working my program as a single person. I learned not to dwell on negativity or amass resentment. I learned how to protect myself, how to express myself, and when to keep my thoughts to myself.

I recently remarried and every day I do my best to handle problems in a positive way, let go when necessary, and accept my mate. Today my life is 95% good times. CoDA has taught me to let go, get on with my life, and grab the best life offers. I deserve it!

# AUGUST 31

# *In This Moment,*
# *I am balanced.*

When I feel overwhelmed and stressed out, I am forgetting my divine heritage — that I am a child of God. I am a spiritual being having a human experience. I am protected and infinitely loved by God. I am centered, grounded to the earth, and committed to being alive. I choose my path. My choices serve and protect my highest good. I am responsible for being in the present and living each moment to the fullest. I take care of myself and am happy to be here.

# SEPTEMBER 1

# *In This Moment,*
# *I'm thankful for lessons.*

I believe God sends people into my life to teach me lessons. I've learned a lot. People are not always who I think they are. In fact, they are not always who they say they are. I no longer take a little information and invent the rest. I now take time to get to know and accept people as they really are, not as I imagine them. As I've grown in the CoDA program, I've gained a better understanding of who I am and what I need. Today, my relationships are less painful and more real.

# SEPTEMBER 2

## *In This Moment, I set priorities.*

I am overwhelmed. I have committed to do too much. It doesn't matter whether the cause is my desire to please, or my belief that nobody else can do things as well as I can. The end result is the same. There is too much for me to do. My codependent traits have led me into this situation and now I need to prioritize. I want to decide which things I can attend to today. I want to accept challenges more thoughtfully and limit my commitments to the ones I love most. I recite the *Serenity Prayer* more often as I learn to "know the difference."

# SEPTEMBER 3

## *In This Moment, I listen to my inner voice.*

Life is so busy and structured that it's often difficult to keep my healing in mind during the work day or with my family. When I realize that I've been functioning on automatic pilot and my tension is jaw-grindingly high, I look up at the ceiling to break the spell of the everyday world. I remember that I have choices in each day, each chore, each situation. With my glance upward, I affirm that divine guidance is mine. All I have to do is listen.

# SEPTEMBER 4

# *In This Moment, I'm entirely ready.*

I ask God to remove my self-righteousness. Even though I may be right much of the time, it's amazing how little my "rightness" is appreciated by others. In many instances, I need to ask myself, "Would I rather be right or would I rather be happy?" More often than not, I can't have it both ways. Recently, after an aggravating situation at work, I prayed about Step Six. I was surprised to find the bitterness gone from my heart within a short time. I reviewed the situation — would the feelings return? When they didn't materialize, I expressed gratitude to my Higher Power. Why had I waited so long? It's so simple.

# SEPTEMBER 5

# *In This Moment,*
# *I am grateful for Step Three.*

By working the Steps, I've learned that my Higher Power does care about me physically, mentally, and spiritually. The God of my understanding cares about who I am, what I do, and how I feel. When I turn my will and my life over to the care of my Higher Power, I experience unconditional love. Little miracles appear in my life. I feel loved, special, and worthwhile.

# SEPTEMBER 6

## *In This Moment, I don't give up.*

I don't give up, I let go; two different things. Giving up means I don't try. I resign myself that I'll never get what I want and abandon hope. I now believe I deserve good things and some day I'll have them. I let go of the timetable, let go of making it happen, let go of control. I may be living in humble circumstances, yet I hope for better. I do what's in my power today to reach my goals. Like getting up and going to work. I may have few decent outfits, and I look forward to the day when I will buy some new clothes. Today, strength and dignity are my clothing.

# SEPTEMBER 7

## *In This Moment, I embrace my history — the joy and the pain.*

I do not condemn my past, stay stuck in it, or run away from it. To genuinely be myself, I must integrate my past wholly. It is part of who I am today, but it is not all that I am. I honor those who have been my teachers for the lessons, even if they were painful at the time. By embracing my past fully, I am freed to make choices in my present. Each day, I have the opportunity to create a new life. I use the lessons that I've learned to make every day better.

# SEPTEMBER 8

# *In This Moment,*
# *I'm free from worry and stress.*

I spent most of my life thinking that I actually have control over every aspect of my life. I've lost many nights of sleep, worrying about things over which I had no control. Step Three tells me to turn my will and my life over to the care of God. It sounds so simple, yet for me, it is my greatest challenge. I am at a point in my recovery where I realize I have no other option but to work Step Three. I only imagined that I was in control. Now, I turn my will over to a caring and loving Higher Power. Letting go frees me from worry and stress. I sleep better.

# SEPTEMBER 9

## *In This Moment, I accept who I am.*

I was having difficulty with a new job that wasn't going well. I kept trying to make it better. I wanted my bosses and co-workers to think well of me and had aligned myself with what I thought was their opinion of me, rather than trusting in my Higher Power's will for me. When I realized that I am just mismatched for this job, I accepted that I am worthwhile even if I can't do this particular job well. I am now looking for a position that better suits my skills. Little by little, I am consciously becoming myself.

# SEPTEMBER 10

# *In This Moment, I matter.*

A golfer asked his partner, "What's your handicap?" to which the partner responded, "My childhood." I laughed! Is it funny? No! Do I relate? You betcha! Feeling unloved, unwanted, unworthy, that's the result of my childhood, thus my handicap. This is at the heart of all my hurts. Can I ever make it go away? I can! It means working on undoing that mind set, rejecting that belief. Affirmations are good for me. I do them daily. I keep my CoDA affirmation booklet at my desk at work. That's when and where I need it most. Today's affirmation — my favorite: I MATTER.

# SEPTEMBER 11

## *In This Moment, I choose color.*

Before recovery, my world was monochromatic, a vision of darkness and gloom. The world seemed meaningless.

In recovery in CoDA, I received my Higher Power's invitation to a new life. I left hopelessness and victimhood behind. My Higher Power encourages me to see reds and blues, greens and golds, to hear music and laughter, to experience unconditional love, and to be present in each moment. Now, I have balance in my life. There is sadness and joy. Hard times and easy ones. I work and play. I spend time alone and time with others. The world offers me more wonders than I can imagine.

# SEPTEMBER 12

## *In This Moment, I feel tired.*

I worked hard today. I experienced stress and tension in my relationships with CoDA friends. During a meeting, I clenched my jaw and dug my nails into the palms of my hands. Before recovery, I might have felt guilt or shame at the end of such a day. In CoDA recovery, I have received gifts which support me to act in healthier ways. I affirm my powerlessness over others. I do a quick inventory in the afternoon to see if I need to admit to any wrongs. I remind myself that I am one among equals. Each deserves a chance to be heard. Even though I'm tired after a long day, no one needs caretaking. I'm at peace with myself. I did the best I could and let go.

# SEPTEMBER 13

# *In This Moment,*
# *I let go of my need for approval.*

There are occasions in my life when I think I need the love and approval of another person to feel good about myself. Any form of rejection only verifies my feeling of low self-worth and starts me on a spiral of negativity and depression. My Step Four inventory opens my eyes to this harmful cycle. My situation will not change until I change.

With the help of my Higher Power, who loves and cares for me, I am learning to love and value myself, including my feelings, thoughts, opinions, and beliefs. Gradually, outside approval becomes less important, and I begin to see myself as valuable and strong.

Today, I work on loving and valuing myself. As my need for approval from others decreases, my level of happiness increases. I view myself as a whole, lovable person.

# SEPTEMBER 14

# *In This Moment,*
# *I accept my codependence.*

When I first came to CoDA and heard the line in the *Welcome* about codependence being "a most deeply rooted, compulsive behavior," I thought, "Not for me." While I could easily admit to some relationship issues, believing that codependence was a compulsion made me sound so, well, powerless.

Today, I understand that admitting powerlessness needn't be admitting defeat. Instead, it's a step toward self-acceptance and self-awareness. Now, when I'm at a meeting and I hear about this "deeply rooted, compulsive behavior," I apply it to myself without shame. I am a codependent, gratefully recovering one day at a time.

# SEPTEMBER 15

## *In This Moment, I awaken.*

One day I asked myself if I had really changed, if my life was working better in ways that count. I was working my program every day, but where were the bells and whistles I'd come to expect? Where was the thunderbolt coming down from heaven with my great big spiritual awakening?

There was only me. There was only today. As I looked deeper, I began to see the small, countless ways I had integrated my program into my life. When I let go and let God, my program was effortless — it was working me. I hardly noticed.

It has been a long, slow, gradual awakening, but miraculous nonetheless. My body and my soul are waking up. My eyes are wide open and I see the light. My Higher Power is everywhere in my life. I find a new depth of wisdom, a new awakening. It is enough.

# SEPTEMBER 16

# *In This Moment,*
# *I see myself honestly.*

Most of my life I thought I was a victim. Poor me. Now I know that the real victimizer lived inside me. I believed that fairy tale about a wedding, a cozy home, healthy children, and "happily ever after." As I struggled to fulfill an unrealistic dream, my real life was miserable. When I hit bottom, a good friend took me to a CoDA meeting. As soon as I heard the Steps and felt the love, I knew my Higher Power was at work. I began to see that I could have made better choices. I had victimized myself, but I vowed "Never again!" With patience and support, I work my CoDA program to keep me strong.

# SEPTEMBER 17

## *In This Moment, I consider the needs of others in a new way.*

I have prided myself on helping other people and sometimes became upset with them when they showed a lack of appreciation. I felt angry if they didn't thank me profusely. Through CoDA, I now recognize that I have made a habit of providing help without checking first. Now, instead of plunging ahead, I ask first. My life is so much simpler.

# SEPTEMBER 18

## *In This Moment, I take my time.*

When I hurry to get things done, I often make mistakes which take extra time to correct. This frustrates me and puts me further behind. Before recovery, I wasn't aware of the negative cycle I created. Nor did I take responsibility for the attitude I adopted.

Now, when I'm feeling rushed, I remind myself; "the hurrier I go, the behinder I get." That simple phrase changes my mood, slows me down, and causes me to smile. I'm more likely to do things in a timely manner and, as a result, feel a whole lot better about myself.

# SEPTEMBER 19

# *In This Moment,*
# *I release resentments.*

I want to let go of resentments for my own healing. It's not about punishing anyone else. Resentments only hurt me, not the other person. They keep me stuck in the past. Resentments can also be powerful teachers. They show me where I need to heal, but when I wallow in past hurts, I rob myself of the present moment. I release them with my Higher Power's help.

# SEPTEMBER 20

## *In This Moment, I'm remorseful.*

My whole body reacted. I felt hurt, which instantly turned to fear, which then shifted into blame. All in a couple of seconds. Why? The tone of an e-mail reminded me of my father's too loud, angry voice. Instead of stopping to think, I sent an immediate, reactive answer. What a slip into codependence!

In my recovery, I don't want to be controlled by my fears. I want to be aware of my triggers so I can act, rather than react. I want to admit — promptly — when I make a mistake.

Higher Power, please guide me and help me to heal.

# SEPTEMBER 21

## *In This Moment,
I live for today.*

I am a happy child of God. This way of thinking hasn't always been easy for me. I have to remind myself to live in the moment. I set boundaries on the "committee in my head." I stop obsessing over, "what if," "I can't," or "I shouldn't."

When I am open to my Higher Power's will, my mind becomes free of the old tapes. I learn new messages. When I am relaxed and calm, I find the joy of living in peace, the meaning of true serenity in my mind, body, and spirit. I don't fret about tomorrow. I live for today.

# SEPTEMBER 22

# *In This Moment, I respect my body.*

When my body speaks through aches and pains or illness, I now listen to it and take steps to nurture and heal it. How many times have I pushed myself beyond my physical limits — getting exhausted or sick? How often have I ignored or denied my body's responses and pleas? I don't have to wait until my body gives out and forces me to rest and take care of it.

I am now proactive in caring for my body. I eat healthy, nurturing foods, get enough rest, exercise regularly, and keep away from harmful and toxic substances. My body thanks me!

# SEPTEMBER 23

# *In This Moment, I'm learning.*

CoDA has taught me many lessons. My immediate reactions used to be fueled by the anger I'd accumulated over the years. My reactions were often over-reactions. Now, I am trying to respond appropriately rather than react with anger. But the lessons haven't fully taken hold. I'm still learning to use my new recovery tools. In the meantime, I need to temper my reactions. I remember the ironic guidance, "Don't just do something, stand there." What a good idea!

# SEPTEMBER 24

## *In This Moment, I make decisions.*

I was often belittled and unsupported for decisions I'd made. I had little adult support and almost no confidence or self-esteem. I didn't know I could give myself a break and learn and grow from whatever decisions I made.

Not making decisions seemed to be a safer, easier path than suffering the consequences of making a poor one. Avoiding decisions became my norm.

In recovery, I understand that making decisions takes courage and effort. I choose to go beyond staying stuck in the past. For me to be living my life fully means that I need to ask myself the hard questions and make the hard decisions.

# SEPTEMBER 25

## *In This Moment, I am powerless.*

When my ex-boyfriend said, "Nothing you could have done would have changed things," I realized I am powerless to make anyone love me and want to commit. However, being powerless also means I'm not responsible because someone doesn't love me. At most, my failure was staying with unavailable and unloving partners.

Admitting I am powerless to affect another's love and commitment doesn't mean those things are impossible. If it's God's will, it will happen in God's time. In my powerlessness lies my hope for a loving, committed relationship.

# SEPTEMBER 26

## *In This Moment, recovery kicks in.*

Controlling? Me?

I still want to control people and things over which I have absolutely no power. I know it doesn't make sense, but it's hard to break this ingrained pattern. Right now, I want to control my partner's nail-chewing anxiety. Earlier today, I wanted to control a rush-hour traffic jam. What a pointless waste of my energy!

Sooner or later, recovery kicks in. I admit my powerlessness and turn it over. It's the only way to live and love.

# SEPTEMBER 27

# *In This Moment, I focus on me.*

My focus used to be on others. I was a talented people-pleaser. I thought I knew what everyone else wanted, needed, and felt. Now, in CoDA, I am looking at myself: my behaviors, my feelings, my issues. I am learning to love and take care of myself. I no longer do the same things over and over and expect different results. CoDA has shown me a path out of insanity. The Fifth Promise has come true: "I feel genuinely lovable, loving, and loved."

# SEPTEMBER 28

## *In This Moment, I have fun.*

I've discovered the "fun" in "dysfunctional" through service work on a CoDA committee. Discussing ideas is creative, challenging, and fun.

While I'm having fun, I continue to learn: to honor group conscience decisions, to take constructive criticism without getting upset, to set boundaries, to express my opinions without malice, to be flexible — even if it means working until midnight.

While I'm learning, I'm still having fun exchanging stories, laughing, acting silly, sharing fabulous desserts. I feel a part of this group. I laugh a lot. I have fun.

# SEPTEMBER 29

# *In This Moment, I establish new patterns.*

Old patterns hurt me and held me back. I now practice new behaviors. I protect, nurture, support, and love myself. I listen to the wisdom of my spiritual self. I take care of my body — giving myself proper rest, relaxation, exercise, and nutrition. I communicate my thoughts to others in loving ways. I open my heart and let others in. I choose to be alive.

# SEPTEMBER 30

# *In This Moment, I choose my spiritual family.*

Although I love my blood relatives, they can't always understand and support the changes in me. Even if my parents can't give me the love I deserve, my needs are still valid. It's my responsibility to ensure my needs are met. I have a legitimate need for encouragement as I grow in recovery. How others treat me is more often a reflection of them than of me. Hurt people hurt people. Loving people are loving to others. As it says in Tradition Three, "The only requirement for membership is a desire for healthy and loving relationships." It's my job to find and nurture those positive relationships and create my own spiritual family.

# OCTOBER 1

# *In This Moment, I love and accept.*

Sometimes, I focus on the fact that not many others seem interested in doing service work. Then I stop and realize that's not my concern. I only have control over myself, no one else. I've been doing service work on many different levels: local, state, and world. There are often many challenges. Sometimes, I feel overwhelmed and unappreciated. I use my program, the Steps, and Traditions to help me recognize and address my conflicting issues of control and people-pleasing. As I learn, I'm becoming a better person. Life is easier and I'm easier to live with. I do service work for myself, to continue improving my experience, strength, and hope. I can't picture myself without it.

# **OCTOBER 2**

# *In This Moment, I know what others think of me is none of my business.*

Worrying about what others think of me keeps me stuck in people-pleasing and impression-management. I can never really rest. I'm in someone else's head!

I go deep within myself and ask, "What do I think and what do I want to do?" Then I find the clear path.

# OCTOBER 3

## *In This Moment, I am recovering.*

I'm open and willing to grow in recovery. I can't do this overnight and I can't do this alone, but I can do this. By consistently taking small, baby steps, one day at a time, I make progress.

I've learned that this is a "we" program, not a "me" program. With my Higher Power's guidance and the help of others in recovery, I can do what I can't do alone.

# **OCTOBER 4**

# *In This Moment,*
# *I thank God.*

At work recently, I became enraged when a staff member canceled an appointment I had made for a client. I screamed inwardly. Then I hammered out a note to my boss and left it on my desk while I went to a doctor's appointment. In the waiting room, I glanced at the horoscope in the paper, something I seldom do. Under my sign I read, "Your mother always said 'Think before you speak.' Remember that in your dealings today." I had to laugh. When I returned to work, the staff member approached me and explained why he had canceled the appointment. It made sense. Thank you, God, for unsent letters and unspoken words.

# OCTOBER 5

# *In This Moment, I want to know God's will.*

Sometimes, I question myself. Am I praying in the right way? I compare myself with what others tell me about how they work Step Eleven. What if I'm doing it wrong? Then I remember to "Keep it Simple." I pray, "God, please let me know your will for me and please give me whatever I need to carry it out." Said on a daily basis, this prayer connects me to God. I trust that whatever happens, I'll be all right. All I have to do is show up and be willing.

# OCTOBER 6

# *In This Moment,*
# *I open my eyes.*

I open my eyes to see the blessings of this day. Often, they aren't the blessings I'm desperately praying for. Sometimes I'm preoccupied, trying to make things happen. Then I might overlook these special gifts: a sunset, a warm moment with a friend, a genuine compliment or word of thanks, finding just the right bargain. Life is rich with blessings and gifts from God.

# OCTOBER 7

## *In This Moment,*
## *I let go of resistance.*

Sometimes, I am dismayed that the biggest obstacle in my path is myself. I am my own worst enemy, allowing fear (real or imagined) to block my way to happiness and success. I used to believe that I didn't deserve all the good things in life and continued to wallow in misery.

In recovery, I learn to recognize patterns of self-sabotage as I'm about to grab the brass ring. I realize there is nothing I must, should, or have to do. Instead, I let go of resistance and allow the flow of the universe to bring joyful experiences into my life.

# OCTOBER 8

# *In This Moment, I am serving CoDA.*

I am in a literature committee meeting at a CoDA Service Conference. There are three new members here; their excitement is contagious. Serving on this committee has spurred my growth in the last four years. By sharing recovery in the written work and in committee meetings, I have come to understand the concepts of CoDA as never before. I use that wisdom in many aspects of my life. I know myself better. I see others more clearly. I make healthier decisions. I feel good.

# OCTOBER 9

# *In This Moment, I ask God to remove my shortcomings.*

I grew up in a home where very little direct, honest communication was heard. I learned to avoid truthful conversations. I learned that it was not safe to speak directly to someone who had violated my boundaries. Many times, I resorted to talking behind a family member's back.

Today, I sometimes fall back into this old behavior of not speaking directly to someone who has treated me inappropriately. When I become aware that this pattern is recurring, I ask God to remove this defect of character. I ask for the courage to speak up when it is appropriate to do so. If I need a reality check, I speak to my sponsor or a trusted CoDA friend.

Having humbly asked God to remove my shortcomings, I relax and let go.

# OCTOBER 10

## *In This Moment,*
## *I admit I was wrong*
## *and amend my behavior.*

I have made a mistake and have hurt others and myself by my codependent acts. I could feel guilty and ashamed and beat myself up, but that does not help anyone. Instead, I take a deep breath, admit my mistake, let go of trying to influence other people's opinions of me, and go forward. Step Ten gives me permission to be human and imperfect and tells me what to do next. Admit it. I can't change the past. Instead of hating myself, I forgive myself. I say, "I'm sorry," and start over.

# OCTOBER 11

## *In This Moment, I make amends to myself.*

As a codependent, I ultimately caused much harm to myself. Controlling others, striving for perfection, and isolating are patterns of my codependency. When I read Step Nine, I realize that the most important person I need to make amends to is myself. I am a precious creation. Yes, I make mistakes, but now I realize that I am not alone. I am not responsible for anyone else's feelings or attitudes, only my own. I lovingly forgive myself.

# OCTOBER 12

# *In This Moment,*
# *I admit I am powerless.*

I do Step One often — many times a day. When things aren't going the way I think they should, I admit I'm powerless. It's frustrating. Sometimes, I want to scream. But if I think about it — there are eleven other Steps available to me. The one I usually choose is Step Three. I let go and let God. I feel a whole lot better.

# OCTOBER 13

## *In This Moment, I use boundaries effectively.*

If my boundaries are weak, chaos, misunderstanding, and hurt occur. When my boundaries are strong, serenity, understanding, and love are more likely to occur. When I set a boundary, I express my reality clearly. I use "I" statements and describe my feelings and perceptions without blaming or shaming. When I listen, I let others express their reality without reacting. I do not give advice.

As I continue to establish boundaries, my relationships become healthier. My new friendships are formed with healthy, functional people.

# OCTOBER 14

## *In This Moment,*
## *I release my fears of being judged.*

I choose to forgive myself and avoid projecting my feelings of inadequacy onto others. I allow myself to be fully human by learning from my mistakes and growing in recovery. I take mature ownership and personal responsibility for my own thoughts, emotions, and actions.

I know a new freedom when I release myself from shame and guilt. I accept unconditional love, peace, and forgiveness from my Higher Power.

# OCTOBER 15

# *In This Moment, I am not alone.*

I have been spending a lot of time with other CoDA members in the last week. It's great! We are each different, but not terminally unique. We have many experiences in common. Today, I know I'm not a misfit or a weirdo. I feel courageous because I am working my program, looking at myself, and making changes. Recovery isn't easy, but it sure helps knowing that there are others out there doing the same. I've heard in meetings, "No one recovers alone." Now, I know that's true.

# OCTOBER 16

# *In This Moment,*
# *I'm finally learning.*

For years, I thought I intuitively understood what another person was thinking or feeling, and that I was right to assume that how I interpreted their actions and words was exactly what they intended to convey.

What I learned from experience is that I never know what is going on in another person's life or mind at any given time. When I feel someone is responding or reacting inappropriately, I need to allow them to be who they are at that moment. Not everything is about me. Life has its ups and downs and emotions are triggered by those ebbs and flows. I'm finally learning that I am not in control. That's OK; God is.

# OCTOBER 17

# *In This Moment, I envision my goals.*

For many years, I lived out the goals of other people — my parents, teachers, or even society at large. Today, I am clear on what I want to experience and how I want to live my life. I see my long-range goals, but I also break them down into more manageable bite-size chunks so they don't become too overwhelming. I could never seem to save up $1,000 to invest, but I can save $25 or $50 a month. Losing 50 pounds seems insurmountable, but I can go to the gym 2-3 times a week for 30 minutes. Little steps add up over time. My goals are specific, measurable, achievable, and have a realistic timeline. I can do this.

# OCTOBER 18

## *In This Moment, I value myself.*

For many years, my parents were majority stockholders in my personal corporation — the one in my head. They didn't even need to vote or express an opinion. I just went ahead and made the decisions that I assumed they would like. I lived my life codependently, trying to satisfy their unspoken standards.

As it says in our CoDA *Welcome,* I found a new freedom from my self-defeating lifestyle. Today, I value myself. I decide what is best for me.

# OCTOBER 19

# *In This Moment, I relax.*

In many meetings I have attended, the topic has been fear. Before I came to CoDA, fear meant, "Forget Everything and Run." In recovery, it's changed to, "Face Everything and Recover." I know when fear comes up, I have a choice. I can react or I can act. These days, I choose to act. I acknowledge the fear, practice positive self-talk, write about it, and share with my sponsor. Then I let it go, and I relax.

# OCTOBER 20

# *In This Moment, I am not afraid.*

To live this day only, not tackling all my problems at once;
To be happy;
To accept what is, not wish things were different;
To take care of myself;
To work my program as I understand it;
To reach out to another person;
To have time to pray and meditate with my Higher Power;
To enjoy what is good and beautiful in life;
To believe the CoDA Promises will come true.

In this moment, my thoughts dance freely and my spirit soars.

I thank my Higher Power for granting me this moment.

# **OCTOBER 21**

# *In This Moment,*
# *I rejoice in the Fellowship.*

Someone once said, "Don't look back — something might be gaining on you!" My bad habit used to be looking ahead, expecting to see trouble coming around the corner. I never did anything about it and whether it actually arrived or not, I wore myself out worrying. Not only that, I often missed good things that were happening in the only real time, which is NOW.

At a recent CoDA meeting, I was lost in worry about the future. A friend brought me back to the present with a "hello" and a hug.

# OCTOBER 22

# *In This Moment,*
# *I set priorities.*

I woke up this morning feeling overwhelmed. There are so many things on my mental "to do" list and I think everything must be done today. Recovery has taught me to do a reality check, so I take a deep breath and honestly assess this long list.

Once my fears are calmed, I begin to prioritize items. Some are important and need to be taken care of as soon as possible, but most can wait for another day.

I begin my day by dealing with one thing at a time, in their order of importance.

# OCTOBER 23

## *In This Moment, I feel sadness.*

Daddy worked into his eighties. Then he started having problems orienting himself. In a short time, he had to stop working and driving. He has dementia. On the outside he looks like my father. On the inside, well, I just don't know what's going on inside him these days. Thank God for my years in CoDA. Thanks to recovery, I let go of wanting Daddy to be different. I accept my father as he is, a man who is often frustrated and sometimes drinks, who loves my mother and me very much, who cares deeply for family and friends. Once, I asked my father if he had faith. He said, "No." Because of my recovery, I know that Daddy has a Higher Power even if he doesn't realize it. I know my Higher Power will guide me through this difficult time.

# OCTOBER 24

# *In This Moment,*
# *I know to reach for the oxygen!*

On a recent trip, a flight attendant instructed us, "In an emergency, put the oxygen mask on yourself first. Then you will be able to help others." This made sense in an airplane — and in my life. When I was growing up, everyone else's needs came first. As an adult, I continued to put myself last. Trying to take care of everyone else was overwhelming. I lost myself. My life was unmanageable.

In CoDA, I'm learning to put my own needs first. I accept my Higher Power's guidance. In a crisis, I reach for the oxygen first. I'm confident that my Higher Power keeps it within easy reach.

# **OCTOBER 25**

# *In This Moment,*
# *I choose.*

Now that I'm recovering from codependence, I make decisions in my life based on what I think is important, not what other people say I "should" do. I know what my values are. I decide how I want to spend my time and live my life according to those values. I have clearly defined goals. I am an adult, capable of taking care of myself and meeting my own needs. My conscious choices further my goals and fill my spirit.

# OCTOBER 26

# *In This Moment,*
# *I respond respectfully.*

If someone treats me critically, negatively, or disrespectfully, it's not because I deserve such treatment. I don't need to take their inventory, nor do I need to buy into their opinion. How I react to other people speaks volumes about me, my history, and my communication skills. By going to CoDA meetings, I'm learning how to speak up, set limits, and still be respectful of others.

# OCTOBER 27

# *In This Moment,*
# *I am committed to my recovery.*

For me, commitment is a living, breathing thing. It is a conscious choice that I make today and every day. I commit to myself first before I commit to others. Only if I take care of myself can I have healthy relationships or be of service to others. Then genuine love and energy flow.

# OCTOBER 28

# *In This Moment, I'm changing.*

I used to weigh everything I said to my lover. I was afraid to ask questions. I picked men with whom I felt inferior and then I'd feel less than. I used to think that if only I found the right person I wouldn't have to pretend or imagine.

Today, I need to be true to myself. Discovering this is part of my recovery. I work my program to change what needs to change — me.

# OCTOBER 29

# *In This Moment, I receive.*

I recently had an opportunity to travel alone. I researched the local attractions and read up on the public transportation system. That was the easy part. The difficulty was in leaving the security of the hotel to walk half a mile to the trolley stop, figuring out how to purchase a day pass from a machine, and deciding which side of the tracks to wait on. I had to ask for help, something I haven't always been comfortable doing.

I learned to reach out to others through recovery. Reaching out to strangers is challenging, but I find that people often go above and beyond in their efforts to help. It is a humbling, yet eye-opening experience to be on the receiving end of giving.

# **OCTOBER 30**

# *In This Moment,*
# *I embrace change.*

Change is often uncomfortable and scary. Some days, I'd rather stay in bed and hide under the covers than deal with the changes I know I need to make. Often, change can be good — just unfamiliar. It helps to remember that if I make a change and don't like it, I can try something else. Sometimes, when I run from change, life situations occur that require change, whether I'm ready or not. When I embrace change and move into the new flow, my life improves in ways that I couldn't have imagined. I trust that through my Higher Power, the changes I face will bring lessons that encourage me to grow and experience life more fully.

# OCTOBER 31

# *In This Moment,*
# *I am challenged by perfectionism.*

Too often, I struggle to complete my tasks perfectly, even though I know that perfection is impossible. I concentrate on the need for a perfect work product, forgetting that, "good enough" is good enough. A less than perfect product may be adequate. It's about progress, not perfection.

# NOVEMBER 1

## *In This Moment, I seek conscious contact with God.*

If I have to pick a favorite Step, it's Step Eleven. When I came into the program, I was hungry to know God. Through prayer and meditation, I journey inward and no longer feel eternally lost. The more I practice meditation, the more deeply I want to know God. I am captivated. At the end of my first year in CoDA, I see a huge difference in my life. No more feeling disconnected. No more chaos. I love the CoDA program.

# NOVEMBER 2

# *In This Moment,*
# *I'm turning it over.*

My home meeting may close. I've attended regularly since I discovered CoDA thirteen years ago; it's the first meeting I ever went to. I discovered a new life in that room and my life is better because of it.

I've gone regularly this year even though there were nights I didn't feel like going. I went because the meeting is smaller and I don't want it to fold. I want the meeting to be there for me and for other suffering codependents.

I'm grateful for all those Tuesday evenings and the people who shared. I'm powerless over the outcome. I've done what I can.

Now, I let go and turn it over to my Higher Power.

# NOVEMBER 3

# *In This Moment,*
# *I own my courage.*

I am no longer caught in "paralysis by analysis." I take action. If I find one action doesn't lead me to my goals, I correct my course. I have the willingness to let go of everything dragging me down and holding me back. Even if I feel afraid, I put one foot in front of the other and do what helps me grow in the long run. I don't make life more difficult than it needs to be. I am able to laugh at myself and have fun through this process.

# NOVEMBER 4

# *In This Moment, I ask God to remove my dishonesty.*

Being honest with myself and others happens more frequently and easily when I am in touch with my Higher Power. Relying on God's unconditional love and strength helps me to be emotionally honest with myself and those I love. In working Step Seven, I ask God to remove my dishonesty. I want to become honest. The CoDA workbook on Step Seven reads, "As recovering codependent adults, we ask God to remove our shortcomings, our fears, self-criticism, and perfectionism, and then let go."

I ask God for help and then let go. I trust God to remove my shortcomings as God sees fit. I feel a joyous sense of freedom.

# NOVEMBER 5

# *In This Moment, I value interdependence.*

Somewhere between codependence and independence is a position I call interdependence; two people who depend on each other and who are dependable. People who nurture, encourage, love, and respect each other without keeping score.

I learned in CoDA to work toward healthy and loving relationships. Now, I want interdependent relationships, not codependent ones. Balancing between codependence and independence is a little like walking on a tight rope. When I lean too far toward codependency, I use my CoDA program to regain my balance. If I lean too far to the other side, I remember that love is about forgiving and living in harmony.

# NOVEMBER 6

## *In This Moment, I look at my behavior.*

Tonight, after a meeting, I listened to someone talk and talk and talk some more. I started out being supportive, but then went way beyond empathy and down the path of codependence.

Where was my time boundary? In my head. I could have cut off the conversation after a reasonable amount of time. Now, instead of blaming myself, I'm practicing what to say when it happens again. Excuse me, I need to leave now. Or simply — gotta go.

I can be a good listener without being codependent.

# NOVEMBER 7

# *In This Moment, I do the footwork.*

When I first came to CoDA and heard about acceptance and letting go, I thought "I've been doing that my whole life." I had been "accepting" my family situation and "letting go" of voicing my needs, over and over. This program had nothing new for me!

In a meeting, I heard someone say that in CoDA we do the footwork and let go of the results. I then realized that instead of letting go, I had taken on a victim role. Instead of accepting the situation, I had endured it. Exactly what I had learned from my family of origin!

Now, I rely on my Higher Power for wisdom to know when to take action and when to let go.

# NOVEMBER 8

# *In This Moment, I listen.*

I acknowledge my falsehoods.
I ask for the truth about myself.
As I discover these truths,
My relationship with God grows.

My recovery improves as I
Listen for God's message,
Let it in,
Love myself.

# NOVEMBER 9

## *In This Moment, I sit still.*

When I feel chaotic, anxious, or overwhelmed, I am neglecting myself. I am out of touch with myself and my Higher Power. I need to be still.

I connect with myself by focusing inward and talking to that scared little girl who didn't get what she needed growing up. I stop analyzing everything. I sit still and am one with her feelings. I comfort and love her. I focus on staying in the present and think, what is the next right thing to do? I meditate to know God's will for me. I pray for the power to carry it out. I appreciate the stillness inside me.

# NOVEMBER 10

# *In This Moment,*
# *I have enthusiasm.*

Enthusiasm is that certain something that makes me feel special. My face lights up. I laugh and sing out loud; soon others join in. Enthusiasm helps me feel confident. There's a spring in my step, joy in my heart, and a twinkle in my eye. I become optimistic and it shows. I make friends easily.

I am grateful to CoDA and my Higher Power for the ability to experience life fully.

# NOVEMBER 11

# *In This Moment,*
# *I pray for knowledge of my*
# *Higher Power's will for me.*

I use Step Eleven as a way to practice humility and as a reminder of my decision to turn my will and life over to my Higher Power's care. There are days when everything's spinning out of control; I feel lost, desperate, and insane. At these times, I cling to this Step like a raft in a stormy sea. When I don't know what to do, when I can't think straight because I feel so crazy, when there are no good choices — only different shades of bad ones — I pray.

Then I wait. I trust that I will recognize the answer when it comes and have the courage to act in my own best interest. When I'm open to my Higher Power's will, I hear what I need to hear and find the strength to do what I need to do.

# NOVEMBER 12

# *In This Moment, I accept.*

I start every day the same way. As I brush my teeth, I look at a framed copy of a saying that speaks to me about acceptance being the solution to my problems. It reminds me that I can't change other people. I accept them as they are. Many situations are beyond my control. Not accepting them is like beating my head against a wall, which is pretty silly. I am powerless over others, but that doesn't mean I'm helpless. When I accept, I help myself, my attitude, and my life.

# NOVEMBER 13

## *In This Moment, I define the God of my understanding.*

I know I need help from a Higher Power in my recovery, but it took me a while to find the God of my understanding. Old images of God from my childhood kept getting in the way. Letting go of those scary images was not easy, but once I started building my own definition, I felt the loving presence of a "power greater than" myself. Now, I have a simple test for any new idea. If it causes me to feel bad or think of doing self-destructive things, I know that's my old codependent self, not God as I now understand God. My newly defined Higher Power restores me to sanity.

# NOVEMBER 14

# *In This Moment, I observe.*

I have a cat named Lily and her kitten named Katy. Lily functions on instincts. She feeds, grooms, and protects her young. I learn a lot about instincts from watching this mother cat.

I ask God to help me stay in touch with and trust my instincts.

# NOVEMBER 15

## *In This Moment, I trust my vibes.*

If I'm uncomfortable in a situation or around certain people, I can leave. I don't have to explain or justify my feelings to anyone. I can simply walk away and remove myself from the situation. I am learning to listen to my inner voice and follow through with healthy actions. My spiritual self is wise, but its voice is subtle. I pray and meditate daily — even just a few minutes a day — to increase my conscious contact with my Higher Power. Connecting on a regular basis develops the spiritual "muscles" I need for recovery.

# NOVEMBER 16

# *In This Moment, I leave the past behind.*

I woke after a fitful night spent obsessing about the past and the pain I suffered. I assigned blame to others and plotted revenge. This morning, my CoDA recovery clicked in. I remembered that rehashing the past is a waste of my energy. I cannot change the past. The codependent habits I learned in my early years served me well then. Today, I choose to leave them behind. I look forward to a better future.

# NOVEMBER 17

## *In This Moment, I feel better.*

I'm new to CoDA. I'm affected by other people's moods and behaviors. When my Dad tells me I look pretty, it makes me feel happy. I'd be lying if I said it didn't affect me when my boyfriend gets angry. When my mother criticizes my appearance, I feel hurt and upset. When I was passed over for a promotion, I felt resentful.

Step One indicates that I'm powerless over others. But, when I question why other people seem to have power over me, the response is, "Keep coming back, it works if you work it." I'm told to get a sponsor, go to meetings, and read CoDA literature.

I have to admit that I'm starting to feel better and more connected with people. I look forward to attending meetings. I think I will keep coming back. I've got nothing to lose but my misery!

# NOVEMBER 18

# *In This Moment,*
# *I have serenity.*

In my family, people expressed anger on a daily basis. I thought everyone was angry most of the time. As an adult, I carried on that belief; I was often angry. After I came to CoDA, I did a Fourth Step inventory. As a result, I understood that feeling angry is OK, but acting out isn't. I have become more even tempered and pleasant than I ever thought possible. This is a direct result of being able to "let go and let God." When I let go of my expectations and my anger and let God do for me what I cannot do for myself, I experience serenity.

# NOVEMBER 19

## *In This Moment, I feel supported.*

In CoDA, I find the support I need to help me build courage and face fear. When I catch myself blaming and pointing at others, I'm often in denial about some aspect of my life. I start to see that there is something wrong and maybe it does involve me. I no longer need to exist in a state of denial. With the help of trusted CoDA friends, I look deeper and see how certain situations or behaviors are not good for me. I deal with my issues now. Life is good!

# NOVEMBER 20

# *In This Moment,*
# *I'm procrastinating.*

My procrastination seems unrelenting. Right now I'm writing about my recovery, which is a good thing. But the reason I've chosen to do it now — in this moment — is to postpone having to start the day: phone calls, laundry, food shopping, post office, house cleaning, dry cleaners, raking, and more. There's so much to do — why don't I get started? Delay just makes it harder.

Why do I hang on to this character defect? What's the pay-off for me? I could ask my Higher Power to remove my shortcomings, but I avoid that, too, because I don't feel "entirely ready."

I pray for knowledge of God's will for me and the power to carry that out — promptly!

# NOVEMBER 21

# *In This Moment,*
# *I know I have a Higher Power.*

I say a lot of words that sound like I'm turning over my will and my life, but when things go bad, I still want to run the show. At those times, it feels as if my identity and life are dependent on the very things I can't control. In recovery, I've learned to look to my Higher Power for guidance and support. When stumbling blocks appear in my life, I can trip over them or stand on them to get a better view. It's my choice.

# NOVEMBER 22

# *In This Moment,*
# *I crave chocolate.*

I was brought up with the "food will solve everything" mentality. Fall down? Have a cookie. Relationship problems? Ice cream to the rescue. Bad day at work? Donuts in the break room. However, nothing works as well as chocolate. Rolling good chocolate around in my mouth is as pleasing to me as tasting a fine wine would be to a connoisseur.

I now realize that when I'm craving chocolate there's usually something going on internally; an issue needs to be dealt with. I can still have a treat, but I also need to take some action: call a friend, go to a meeting, connect with my sponsor, or write in my journal. Food doesn't solve my problems.

# NOVEMBER 23

## *In This Moment, I celebrate.*

In recovery, I learn the power of truth. Denial is no longer in charge of my life. Instead of running from fear, I learn to face it, using the tools of the program of Co-Dependents Anonymous. I learn it doesn't happen overnight.

I take delight in feeling cared for and respected in my CoDA family. I am elated by the presence of a Higher Power in my life. I have more energy. I celebrate, as I feel the excitement of a full and positive life.

# NOVEMBER 24

# *In This Moment, I give thanks.*

I heard the doctor say there was a spot on my CT scan which needed follow-up with an MRI. I felt fear and anxiety. I imagined all the dark possibilities of what the test might reveal. I had survived cancer fourteen years ago. Recovery teaches me to stay in the moment, to focus on one day (or one minute) at a time. But I was obsessing. I concentrated on breathing and asked my Higher Power for guidance. It was all I could do. Twenty-four achingly long hours after the test, I heard my doctor's voice on the phone. "Benign," he said. I wished the doctor a Happy Thanksgiving, hung up the phone, and dropped to the floor to thank God.

# **NOVEMBER 25**

# *In This Moment, I detach.*

I chose to walk away from my family of origin—not an easy choice. At first, I felt guilty and disloyal. I physically removed my children and myself from harm's way. I couldn't allow them to suffer the mistreatment I had suffered. But as uncomfortable as I felt divorcing my family of origin, I knew it was necessary. Living by my own values and integrity is the best way to protect my children and myself.

Detachment is a necessary and loving thing to do. Today, my children and I are safe.

# NOVEMBER 26

# *In This Moment, I can.*

When I first came into the CoDA program and heard, "Fake it 'til you make it," I thought it seemed such a dishonest phrase. In recovery, I was trying to discover my true self and not be phony. In time, I realized this slogan helps me walk through my fear of change. When my self-talk is negative and fear overwhelms me, I now focus on the positive aspects of the situation. By acting as if I'm already capable of handling things, little by little, I find that indeed I am. It's one of the mysterious rewards I've received in recovery!

# NOVEMBER 27

## *In This Moment, I accept where I am.*

I respect the journey that I am on. I do not compare the pace or rate of my growth to that of others. I am on my own path. I am exactly where I need to be. I avoid taking other people's inventory and instead look at myself. I focus on the lessons that I need to learn and remember that each person and situation can be my teacher, if I allow them to be. I am open to growth.

# NOVEMBER 28

## *In This Moment, I take calculated risks.*

In my past, I was afraid to take risks. As a child, when I took a risk, I was often punished for it, so I learned that taking risks was not OK. I now realize that playing it safe has greatly limited my choices in life. Going from one extreme to another is not the solution. I take the middle path. I don't have to be foolhardy and dive into a pool without first checking to see if it contains water. I take small steps, small risks, and learn what works for me now. When I spend time thinking about the pros and cons of a problem, I am able to determine what solution is best for me and then act on it.

# NOVEMBER 29

# *In This Moment, I take care of myself.*

I stand up for myself. I speak my truth. Saying "no" allows me greater freedom to say "yes" to what is important to me. I do what I say I will do. I set appropriate boundaries. I follow through. I accept responsibility for myself and meet my intrinsic needs. I am committed to my program and myself.

# **NOVEMBER 30**

# *In This Moment, I play.*

For many years, my inner child was locked away in the dark. Now, I allow my inner child to run, jump, and dance. I give my inner child the unconditional love and validation needed. I am childlike by being open to spontaneity and allowing my creativity to flow through. I have fun while still being responsible for myself, not irresponsible and childish. I am curious and adventuresome. I am grateful for this chance to live freely. I am open to life. I am open to joy.

# DECEMBER 1

## *In This Moment, I appreciate myself.*

I acknowledge my progress and accomplishments. I recognize my gains, large and small, by journaling them. This process helps to validate how much I'm doing for myself. Rewards come as I work my program. I see positive changes in my behaviors and attitudes. I communicate more clearly because I know what I'm feeling. At times, I feel flexible and relaxed. I gain new insights, abilities, and skills. I deal with problems, both at home and in the work place, more effectively. My thoughts are more positive and I rarely engage in negative self-talk. There is hope — and evidence!

# DECEMBER 2

# *In This Moment,*
# *I have a spiritual connection.*

I am scared, worried, and don't know what to do, so I'm working the Eleventh Step. It's one of my favorites. I ask "only for knowledge of God's will" for me and "the power to carry that out." When I listen and am open to being guided, it works! My Higher Power is here. There's no doubt in my mind. I'm so grateful for this Step.

# DECEMBER 3

# *In This Moment,*
# *I focus on just this day.*

"Just for today." What a simple phrase, but so hard to remember! I forget this phrase when I'm overwhelmed, anxious, or projecting. The other day, I was arguing with my teenage son and I could think only negative thoughts about his future. Then the light came on. Be in the moment. I was anticipating. I needed to come back to today's problems and solutions, not the future or past. I let go and focus on today. God keeps me on track, one day at a time.

# DECEMBER 4

# *In This Moment,*
# *I create.*

Instead of concentrating on what's wrong with my life, I focus on what's right. I recognize progress as I work on the areas I still need to improve. I ask myself, "What do I love?" so that my consciousness works towards creating more positive experiences in my life. I believe that whatever I focus on is what I create in my life, even on a subconscious level. I replace negative thoughts and mind chatter with love, encouragement, and wisdom. I am grateful to have the honesty, openness, and willingness necessary to work my program of recovery.

# DECEMBER 5

# *In This Moment, I emerge from denial.*

**D**on't even know I have a problem

**E**mbellish the truth

**N**egative consequences

**I**dentify with others

**A**dmit I have a problem

**L**ying is no longer an option

# DECEMBER 6

## *In This Moment, recovery is a journey.*

Step One tells me I am powerless over others. Step Eleven asks me to "pray only for knowledge of God's will" for me and the power to carry that out. Any power I have comes from God. For me, recovery has been hard at times, but well worth the effort. I believe that recovery is a journey, not a destination. By understanding myself, accepting others, and trusting my Higher Power, I take that journey every day of my life.

# DECEMBER 7

# *In This Moment,*
# *I grow through service work.*

When I first joined CoDA, I was shy, introverted, and uncomfortable speaking in front of others. Over the years, I held various service positions: Group Service Rep, Delegate, and committee member. Performing service allows me to practice new behaviors. Although I am still basically a quiet person, I no longer hesitate to express my opinion. I am comfortable and confident when communicating with others. These behavior changes have carried into the workplace and helped me progress in my career. I started doing service to give back. Turns out, the more I give, the more I receive.

# DECEMBER 8

## *In This Moment, I embrace recovery.*

The Nile? Oh — denial!

Nothing was wrong with me — it was everybody else in my life. But I was the one who felt miserable. Taking my husband's inventory was a full-time job. I couldn't hold a meaningful conversation with my parents. I felt "less than." For a long time, I waited for someone to come along and make me happy.

Then I discovered CoDA, where I identified with the sharing. Oh, so slowly, I learned to accept myself, improve my friendships, and let go of unhealthy relationships. My recovery continues to evolve. It doesn't happen on my schedule, but it happens. My Higher Power is mending me. I embrace the healing.

# DECEMBER 9

# *In This Moment,*
# *I choose my attitude.*

A positive attitude is a good way to start the day. How I perceive events determines the quality of my life. I can stay stuck in self-defeating negativity or look at things positively. For me, the choice is clear. I can't change the past, but in CoDA I've learned to look at my experiences in a new, healthier light. I strive each day to see the good in people, places, and things. I am convinced that the quality of my life depends less on what happens to me and more on how I react to those events. I am in charge of my attitude.

# DECEMBER 10

## *In This Moment, I make healthier choices.*

Even in recovery, I find myself doing too much at times. I overextend myself and stay up late working on things that could easily wait until the next day. Recently, while on vacation, I pushed myself to walk too far, for too long. The result — I spent the rest of my day limping around, wincing with pain.

With recovery comes awareness. I know I have choices. I can keep repeating the same behavior, knowing full well the consequences, or I can gracefully and assertively make healthier choices. Today, I know the importance of self-care.

# DECEMBER 11

# *In This Moment, I'm going home.*

For me, "home for the holidays" meant pain. Old childhood wounds would be reopened, and I would find myself falling into pre-recovery behavior patterns. That shouldn't surprise me. It's familiar territory. I "know" what's going to happen. I could write the script of who would say and do what when I arrived. Too often, it went according to the script.

Now, I have a recovery plan in place before I go home for the holidays. I do things differently. I make "I" statements. I write in my journal. I read CoDA literature. I look for the meetings I can attend. I make a list of people I can call. I say the *Serenity Prayer* with faith in my Higher Power. I find opportunities to escape by myself. Going home feels better now. I can take care of myself, even in dysfunctional family situations. Thank you, Higher Power.

# DECEMBER 12

# *In This Moment,*
# *I am blessed with friends.*

At first, I was reluctant to reach out and trust. I was afraid of rejection. Little by little, I tested the waters, one day at a time, one person at a time. I found acceptance. Trust developed. This is new behavior for me. My recovery friends share honestly. I admire their courage, strength, and faith. I keep coming back.

# DECEMBER 13

## *In This Moment, I wait for clarity.*

Sometimes, expressing anger is dangerous. Often, it makes the situation worse. When I have no safe outlet for my anger, I keep it inside. It helps me to talk with a trusted friend. I write letters to God about my feelings. I do what I can to get my feelings out into the open and wait for the anger to pass. After it is gone, I am able to see the situation with clarity. Then, I decide if I need to take action or need to let go.

# DECEMBER 14

## *In This Moment,*
## *I connect with my Higher Power.*

There are many times when I forget to ask for help. I'm afraid to admit that I don't know what to do. I cause myself so much pain and anxiety. Thanks to CoDA, my Higher Power knocks on the door and says, "Hey, remember me?" Why can't I remember? Why don't I go to my Higher Power before I stress myself out?

Today, I know it takes time to change old behavior patterns. With the Steps, CoDA meetings, service work, and my sponsorship relationships, I am changing. I'm learning not to wait so long. It's OK to ask for help!

# DECEMBER 15

# *In This Moment,*
# *I take responsibility.*

I was accused of a wrongdoing that I did not commit. In the past, I would have felt angry but stuffed it down for fear of the other person's response. I might have spiraled into self-doubt and guilt, groveled for forgiveness, and resented that person. Today, I don't feel guilty if I've done nothing wrong. I'm sorry the other person misunderstood me, but I know his feelings are his own. I take responsibility only for my feelings. CoDA recovery teaches me I'm powerless over others.

# DECEMBER 16

# *In This Moment,*
# *I want a healthy relationship.*

I fall in love with the silent ones and dream dreams they know nothing about. I want a healthy, loving relationship with a man to whom I can say anything and who feels the freedom to do the same. It sounds fine, but I still choose men with whom I do not feel equal and then try to pretend we're on the same wavelength. By continuing to grow in the CoDA program, I may attract a man who is compatible in most ways, someone with whom I can be my authentic self. Meanwhile, I work my program and pray for knowledge of God's will for my life.

# DECEMBER 17

## *In This Moment, my heart is broken.*

I've done it again. I've fallen in love with a man who just wants friendship. Why can't I accept that? Why do I want more?

I can't change another; I can only change myself. I need to let go of expectations. I'm sad, but I know I'm still "somebody" even when "nobody" loves me. I have the love of friends and family members, and most importantly, I'm learning to love myself. That's enough to keep me afloat as my heart mends.

# DECEMBER 18

## *In This Moment, I have no regrets.*

I've made a lot of mistakes in my life. I wasn't the perfect wife, mother, or employee. I lost marriages, jobs, kids. When I walked into my first CoDA meeting, I was pretty low. It took me a long time to accept my past. My experiences are my teachers. The Fourth Promise is true for me today: "I release myself from worry, guilt, and regret about my past and present. I am aware enough not to repeat it."

# DECEMBER 19

# *In This Moment,*
# *I sit amid the chaos of my clutter.*

As usual, the desk is littered with papers. So is the floor. As I glance around, I realize that I need to find a home for a bunch of "stuff." I took a workshop on how to de-clutter, but threw away the handouts, knowing they'd become clutter if I let them stay around.

Is there a spiritual dimension to this problem? I feel powerless over my clutter. I struggle to create order in disorder. I share about this issue with friends in recovery and know I'm not alone. I humbly ask my Higher Power to remove this shortcoming. I can make amends to my spouse and myself, one day at a time, if I put things away and throw things away. I need to work at it — and it works when I work it.

# DECEMBER 20

# *In This Moment,*
# *I give by choice.*

I can only give genuine service when I give freely, by my own choice. If I can only give a little sometimes, that's OK. I cannot give what I do not have. In recovery, I'm aware that I need time to relax, play, pray, and meditate — to go back to the spiritual well and fill my soul. Then, I can give to others out of a feeling of fullness, nurturing, and love, instead of resentment and obligation. I help others more when I first help and love myself.

# DECEMBER 21

## *In This Moment, I look within.*

Whenever I feel disturbed, no matter what the cause, I blame myself. I am a fear-based, shame-based codependent. Sometimes, I'm afraid there won't be enough (money, material goods, love) to go around. At other times, I feel shame, as if I'm about to be found out (that I'm not smart enough, sexy enough, or young enough). My feelings erupt as jealousy, anger, self-pity, and self-loathing. At all costs, I avoid looking within. Instead, I blame others.

In CoDA recovery, I'm learning to take my own inventory. I look at my behaviors by journaling, working with my sponsor, and attending meetings. I gain insight and am willing to change.

# DECEMBER 22

## *In This Moment, I have shortcomings.*

I criticize my husband's driving. I indulge in self-pity. I hide. I'm envious. I settle for too little. Why am I not "entirely ready" for God to remove my shortcomings? What prevents me from asking God to remove them?

Am I afraid of having my life changed? Yes, I dread change. I feel dejected and stuck in a rut, but it's such a familiar rut. So I skip over — or trip on — Steps Six and Seven.

Higher Power, I need help to become entirely ready. Please, help me to reach out and expand my life. Help me to overcome my raging codependency.

# DECEMBER 23

## *In This Moment, I am thinking about the upcoming holidays.*

What better gift could I give someone than a gift of myself? Yet, how do I, as a codependent in recovery, accomplish this without compromising my own or another's boundaries? I need to ensure that I am giving freely, without expectations. For example, I call a friend to let her know I am thinking about her or volunteer for a cause I believe in, even though my time is extremely limited. Before I act, I pay attention to any inner rumblings of discontent to avoid later feelings of resentment or regret.

This holiday season, the most meaningful gift I can give my family is to continue working my recovery program.

# **DECEMBER 24**

# *In This Moment, my family gets along.*

It really hurts to have my children act like strangers with each other, especially since their children love playing together. Once I tried to mend fences, but it backfired and everyone was angry with me. I have learned through CoDA to let things happen in God's time. Tonight, on Christmas Eve, I walked into my son's house and found his brother and him playing pool together; their wives were chatting away with my daughter. All nine of my grandchildren were tearing around the house, so excited to see each other again. That was the best Christmas present ever! Thank you, God.

# DECEMBER 25

## *In This Moment, it's OK to feel feelings.*

My children have been questioning the existence of Santa Claus for some time. I feared they'd be disappointed by the truth and that I would feel badly for hurting them. I realized that I was only postponing the inevitable by stalling. In recovery, I've learned that I need to allow myself and others to hear the truth and feel appropriate feelings in order to experience life fully. I decided to tell them that I was indeed Santa Claus and was surprised to see that it was no big deal for them. They just wanted to know the truth.

# DECEMBER 26

# *In This Moment,*
# *I see the humor in my recovery.*

There was a time in my life, when I felt so deeply depressed, and in such pain, that I thought the hurt would never end. I have learned that, "This too, shall pass." Laughing helps to open my heart. I feel lighter in the world, instead of feeling so burdened with responsibility. I use humor appropriately, instead of deflecting or avoiding my real feelings.

My Higher Power has a fantastic sense of humor. When I allow myself to experience it fully, I see the joy in situations. My laughter is full and genuine.

# DECEMBER 27

# *In This Moment,*
# *love finds me.*

I kept praying for my Higher Power to bring me love. Today, while I was sitting on the couch, my kitten climbed my leg looking to play and receive affection. I realized, in that moment, that love comes in many shapes and forms. God, help me keep my eyes open for all gifts of love.

# DECEMBER 28

# *In This Moment, I believe.*

*Just for today:*
I believe in myself.
I'm honest with myself and others.
I'm responsible for my actions.

*Just for today:*
I love myself. I am enough.
I let go of what I cannot control.
I let others own their own stuff.

*Just for today:*
God is in control.
I'm on the right path.
Life is good.

# DECEMBER 29

# *In This Moment,*
# *I create true friendships.*

Intimacy used to be such a foreign word to me. I was afraid to show others who I really am, fearing rejection or ridicule. From going to meetings and sharing in a safe, accepting environment, I'm learning real intimacy by allowing others to "into-me-see." I've learned that intimacy is a living thing, a journey that requires ongoing nurturing. There are so many places in the world that are harsh and critical. How refreshing it is to know that I have a safe haven in CoDA. Ultimately, my goal is to create a safe, accepting environment inside of me.

# DECEMBER 30

# *In This Moment,*
# *I use my daily inventory*
# *as a springboard for change.*

I watch out for self-pity, self-righteousness, and self-condemnation. I strive for gratitude, humility, and gentleness. I catch myself in dishonesty, impatience, resentment, and false pride. I attempt honesty, patience, forgiveness, and modesty. I am aware of jealousy, laziness, procrastination, and fear. I struggle with generosity, activity, promptness, and trust. No matter how disgusted I may be with myself and my behavior, I take the time to review my day. I am then able, with God's help, to see what direction to take. I am capable of healing.

# DECEMBER 31

# *In This Moment, I honor where I am.*

Sometimes, I throw my hands up in frustration when I look at the messes in my life. Many are of my own doing. Some occur when I allow others to run my life. Either way, I must honor the place where I am, before I can move forward.

If I contribute to a bad situation, I need to accept responsibility for my part. I do have choices, and I prefer to channel my creative energies into positive actions. That's the direction I want my life to take.

# The Twelve Steps of Co-Dependents Anonymous©

1. We admitted we were powerless over others, that our lives had become unmanageable.
2. Came to believe that a power greater than ourselves could restore us to sanity.
3. Made a decision to turn our will and our lives over to the care of God as we understood God.
4. Made a searching and fearless moral inventory of ourselves.
5. Admitted to God, to ourselves, and to another human being the exact nature of our wrongs.
6. Were entirely ready to have God remove all these defects of character.
7. Humbly asked God to remove our shortcomings.
8. Made a list of all persons we had harmed and became willing to make amends to them all.
9. Made direct amends to such people wherever possible except when to do so would injure them or others.
10. Continued to take personal inventory and when we were wrong, promptly admitted it.
11. Sought through prayer and meditation to improve our conscious contact with God as we understood God, praying only for knowledge of God's will for us and the power to carry that out.
12. Having had a spiritual awakening as the result of these Steps, we tried to carry this message to other codependents and to practice these principles in all our affairs.

*\*The Twelve Steps are reprinted and adapted with permission of Alcoholics Anonymous World Services, Inc.*

# The Twelve Traditions of Co-Dependents Anonymous©

1. Our common welfare should come first; personal recovery depends upon CoDA unity.
2. For our group purpose there is but one ultimate authority – a loving Higher Power as expressed to our group conscience. Our leaders are but trusted servants; they do not govern.
3. The only requirement for membership in CoDA is a desire for healthy and loving relationships.
4. Each group should remain autonomous except in matters affecting other groups or CoDA as a whole.
5. Each group has but one primary purpose — to carry its message to other codependents who still suffer.
6. A CoDA group ought never endorse, finance, or lend the CoDA name to any related facility or outside enterprise, lest problems of money, property, and prestige divert us from our primary spiritual aim.
7. Every CoDA group ought to be fully self-supporting, declining outside contributions.
8. Co-Dependents Anonymous should remain forever nonprofessional, but our service centers may employ special workers.
9. CoDA, as such, ought never be organized, but we may create service boards or committees directly responsible to those they serve.
10. CoDA has no opinion on outside issues; hence the CoDA name ought never be drawn into public controversy.
11. Our public relations policy is based on attraction rather than promotion; we need always maintain personal anonymity at the level of press, radio, and films.
12. Anonymity is the spiritual foundation of all our traditions; ever reminding us to place principles before personalities.

*\*The Twelve Traditions are reprinted and adapted with permission of Alcoholics Anonymous World Services, Inc.*

# The Twelve Promises of Co-Dependents Anonymous©

1. I know a new sense of belonging. The feeling of emptiness and loneliness will disappear.

2. I am no longer controlled by my fears. I overcome my fears and act with courage, integrity and dignity.

3. I know a new freedom.

4. I release myself from worry, guilt, and regret about my past and present. I am aware enough not to repeat it.

5. I know a new love and acceptance of myself and others. I feel genuinely lovable, loving and loved.

6. I learn to see myself as equal to others. My new and renewed relationships are all with equal partners.

7. I am capable of developing and maintaining healthy and loving relationships. The need to control and manipulate others will disappear as I learn to trust those who are trustworthy.

8. I learn that it is possible to mend – to become more loving, intimate and supportive. I have the choice of communicating with my family in a way which is safe for me and respectful of them.

9. I acknowledge that I am a unique and precious creation.

10. I no longer need to rely solely on others to provide my sense of worth.

11. I trust the guidance I receive from my higher power and come to believe in my own capabilities.

12. I gradually experience serenity, strength, and spiritual growth in my daily life.

# INDEX

# A

Abandoned
    104, 225
Acceptance
    6, 7, 9, 10, 25, 27, 77, 107, 111, 118, 125, 130,
    141, 160, 164, 172, 187, 203, 219, 239, 253, 258,
    275, 290, 297, 312, 317, 332, 352, 366
Addiction
    165, 193
Affirmation
    35, 41, 43, 108, 143, 218, 232, 247, 254, 256
Alone
    11, 28, 32, 35, 45, 52, 115, 132, 147, 196, 203,
    240, 277, 289, 303
Amends
    70, 80, 118, 210, 212, 285
Anger
    95, 120, 156, 261, 267, 278, 323, 348
Anxiety
    39, 47, 131, 153, 329, 349
Approval
    4, 138, 217, 257
Asking for help
    5, 33, 57, 349

# INDEX

Assertiveness
    15, 84, 92, 300, 334
Attitude
    43, 86, 231, 262, 344
Authentic
    12, 14, 15, 207, 214
Avoidance
    29, 79, 120, 283
Awareness
    4, 14, 56, 76, 79, 88, 100, 104, 142, 205, 234, 241, 264, 345, 355

# B

Balance
    134, 160, 178, 209, 244, 255, 310
Behavior
    5, 77, 91, 92, 113, 120, 126, 132, 134, 152, 163, 173, 180, 194, 206, 224, 258, 271, 273, 283, 284, 311, 322, 345, 346, 365
Blame
    8, 27, 61, 225, 260, 264, 321, 356
Boundaries
    60, 87, 114, 139, 166, 180, 197, 218, 265, 283, 287, 311, 334, 358

# INDEX

## C

Caretaking
  48, 84, 136, 176, 197, 298

Change
  1, 5, 12, 15, 18, 27, 32, 34, 44, 50, 54, 56, 57, 61,
  76, 81, 82, 91, 96, 102, 113, 122, 138, 143, 158,
  163, 164, 184, 187, 190, 212, 216, 217, 231, 255,
  259, 289, 302, 304, 331, 336, 342, 345, 349, 365

Chaos
  65, 105, 156, 226, 239, 287, 354

Character defects
  23, 27, 66, 95, 97, 100, 101, 103, 129, 214, 248,
  283, 309, 325, 357

Choices
  22, 37, 44, 53, 59, 60, 64, 69, 84, 91, 101, 102,
  108, 113, 136, 153, 157, 167, 180, 183, 198, 200,
  213, 214, 226, 236, 247, 255, 273, 274, 293, 299,
  330, 333, 344, 345, 355

Clarity
  79, 112, 156, 168, 173, 348

Codependence
  4, 16, 25, 34, 55, 76, 83, 97, 101, 120, 140, 148,
  161, 162, 163, 166, 194, 206, 217, 226, 258, 261,
  264, 284, 311, 327, 356, 358

# INDEX

Commitment
5, 246, 269, 301, 334
Communication
91, 154, 175, 342
Compassion
26, 99, 173
Consequences
60, 181, 345
Control
10, 24, 39, 69, 134, 136, 139, 146, 152, 155, 191, 219, 252, 270, 275, 285, 290, 326
Courage
22, 70, 114, 268, 308, 324
Criticism
30, 91, 300

Decision-making
29, 51, 59, 69, 119, 162, 168, 170, 200, 237, 240, 268, 292, 299, 316
Denial
31, 42, 126, 151, 202, 324, 328, 340, 343

# INDEX

Depression
> 3, 36, 98, 153, 255, 257, 361

Dysfunction
> 36, 66, 346

Envy
> 129, 191

Expectations
> 27, 111, 235, 259, 295, 323, 352

Faith
> 5, 12, 13, 43, 63, 67, 169, 192, 198, 279, 297

Family
> 106, 130, 154, 197, 221, 274, 297, 359

Family of origin
> 28, 30, 106, 117, 130, 132, 150, 157, 164, 186, 206, 207, 229, 297, 312, 330, 346

# INDEX

Fear
    5, 18, 42, 83, 89, 92, 106, 119, 125, 131, 133, 156, 167, 183, 184, 222, 229, 264, 281, 288, 293, 294, 303, 329, 331, 333, 356

Feelings
    14, 36, 46, 84, 85, 91, 104, 115, 121, 137, 146, 151, 154, 157, 167, 202, 205, 213, 235, 256, 314, 320, 322, 348, 360

Fellowship
    28, 40, 52, 83, 101, 127, 133, 174, 206, 295, 343

Focus
    19, 59, 116, 176, 179, 180, 228, 271, 338, 339

Forgiveness
    26, 103, 107, 160, 211, 234, 285, 288, 365

Freedom
    22, 41, 101, 141, 146, 154, 162, 189, 208, 240, 242, 288, 292

Friendship
    3, 64, 83, 174, 203, 225, 324, 347, 352, 364

Frustration
    24, 136, 179, 262, 286, 366

# INDEX

# G

Gift
  25, 37, 99, 109, 164, 168, 215, 280
Goals
  59, 160, 181, 250, 291, 299, 308
God
  5, 9, 13, 30, 49, 50, 62, 66, 70, 85, 93, 95, 103, 119, 124, 145, 155, 168, 188, 224, 244, 306, 309, 318
God's plan
  35, 156
God's will
  9, 71, 159, 160, 165, 253, 265, 279, 314, 337
Gratitude
  3, 14, 21, 38, 40, 49, 74, 88, 96, 106, 124, 155, 164, 170, 177, 190, 191, 278, 315, 329, 339, 359
Grief
  151, 185, 297
Growth
  34, 44, 112, 113, 120, 137, 155, 177, 194, 214, 231, 255, 261, 277, 282, 288, 308, 342
Guidance
  23, 224, 236, 247, 326, 337
Guilt
  107, 211, 284, 350

# INDEX

# H

Happiness
 15, 75, 83, 102, 144, 183, 265
Healing
 34, 40, 43, 44, 66, 112, 115, 125, 135, 137, 141, 211, 229, 245, 263, 266, 365
Healthy
 57, 64, 150, 152, 173, 206
Higher Power
 1, 7, 10, 20, 22, 33, 39, 40, 51, 54, 62, 63, 70, 74, 80, 109, 127, 133, 142, 151, 164, 171, 203, 223, 226, 237, 249, 252, 255, 304, 316
Holidays
 45, 329, 346, 358, 359, 360
Honesty
 42, 66, 78, 91, 92, 124, 125, 155, 181, 219, 260, 309, 365
Hope
 22, 61, 67, 203, 250, 275, 336
Humility
 155, 210, 216, 303, 316, 365

# INDEX

## I

Inadequacy
 108, 288
Inner child
 149, 230, 314, 335
Insanity
 65, 226, 271, 316
Interdependence
 175, 178, 204, 310
Inventory
 116, 126, 139, 256, 365

## J

Journey
 38, 96, 137, 192, 205, 332, 341
Joy
 2, 14, 43, 171, 183, 185, 230, 265, 335

## L

Laughter
 72, 98, 278, 308, 361

# INDEX

Let go and let God
 19, 24, 63, 66, 77, 222, 323

Letting go
 13, 39, 91, 145, 169, 191, 208, 237, 239, 241, 250, 252, 259, 286, 312, 338, 363

Lessons
 26, 68, 113, 131, 179, 221, 225, 245, 251, 267, 290

Listening
 17, 149, 247, 311, 313, 320

Love
 50, 58, 121, 141, 185, 189, 224, 233, 249, 257, 269, 274, 309, 310, 335, 362

Meditation
 9, 20, 38, 294, 306

Meetings
 17, 55, 73, 74, 120, 125, 127, 147, 164, 203, 213, 227, 258, 295, 307

Miracle
 42, 93, 249

Mistakes
 25, 80, 107, 142, 262, 284, 353

# INDEX

## N

Needs
31, 39, 56, 145, 200, 274, 298
Negativity
30, 50, 106, 154, 180, 195, 236, 243

## O

One day at a time
217, 262, 277, 338, 363
Opportunity
177, 231
Overwhelmed
14, 94, 182, 213, 220, 244, 246, 275, 296, 314

## P

Pain
2, 7, 26, 34, 44, 85, 86, 103, 132, 177, 185, 251, 349
Past
1, 62, 153, 167, 251, 321, 353

# INDEX

Patience
    155, 199, 365
Patterns
    5, 88, 154, 273, 283
Peace
    57, 136, 144, 165, 167, 171, 256, 265, 314
People-pleasing
    15, 35, 188, 219, 257, 271, 276
Perfection
    16, 152, 172, 232, 305
Pets
    6, 319, 362
Positive thinking
    83, 86, 217, 243, 328, 331, 336, 339, 344
Power
    14, 18, 65, 114
Powerlessness
    7, 65, 139, 165, 237, 239, 256, 258, 269, 286, 307, 317, 341, 350
Prayer
    9, 20, 49, 71, 156, 159, 168, 216, 248, 279, 280, 316, 362
Present moment
    55, 62, 109, 131, 153, 195, 251, 363

# INDEX

Priorities
    116, 246, 296
Procrastination
    29, 70, 325
Progress
    100, 140, 165, 178, 277, 336
Promises
    27, 31, 42, 70, 89, 106, 107, 137, 184, 208, 234, 271, 353
Purpose
    123, 223, 240

# R

Reaching out
    115, 145, 303
Reacting
    138, 173, 264, 267, 290, 300
Reality
    7, 16, 78, 188, 287, 360
Recovery
    2, 3, 11, 24, 25, 32, 43, 57, 73, 82, 95, 141, 155, 161, 163, 192, 199, 221, 230, 236, 243, 274, 277, 288, 301, 306, 321, 328, 331, 343, 346, 358

# INDEX

Regret
    55, 107, 157, 181, 232
Rejection
    56, 257, 347
Relationships
    6, 8, 23, 27, 40, 45, 57, 130, 140, 163, 178, 188, 189, 204, 225, 245, 256, 274, 287, 310, 351
Resentment
    55, 163, 213, 243, 263
Responsibility
    18, 79, 91, 146, 200, 242, 245, 287, 334, 335, 350

## S

Sadness
    132, 297, 307, 352
Sanity
    72, 131, 220, 226, 318
Self-care
    26, 31, 64, 132, 150, 172, 176, 227, 240, 245, 271, 298, 303, 345
Self-confidence
    32, 67, 144, 238, 268

# INDEX

Self-defeating
    172, 281, 292
Self-esteem
    15, 48, 101, 196, 214, 232, 258, 336
Self-love
    11, 58, 68, 182, 233, 266, 271, 363
Self-pity
    12, 124, 132, 357, 365
Self-righteousness
    248, 365
Self-talk
    195, 217, 254, 293, 331
Self-worth
    25, 113, 135, 257
Serenity Prayer
    19, 24, 122, 231, 246, 270, 346
Serenity
    31, 49, 54, 57, 156, 265, 323
Service
    147, 215, 238, 272, 275, 282, 342, 355
Shame
    73, 119, 142, 172, 218, 284, 288, 356
Shortcomings
    100, 214, 248, 283, 309, 325, 354, 357

# INDEX

Spiritual
  41, 51, 67, 135, 155, 212, 215, 223, 244, 259, 274, 320

Sponsor
  20, 73, 80, 97, 100, 103, 115, 129, 175, 201, 216, 283, 293, 322, 349

Step One
  10, 65, 269, 286, 322, 341

Step Two
  10, 54, 220, 226, 318

Step Three
  7, 10, 19, 22, 39, 63, 77, 124, 145, 165, 195, 198, 203, 222, 249, 252, 286, 323

Step Four
  50, 66, 100, 103, 116, 126, 209, 214, 257, 323

Step Five
  66, 118, 175, 214

Step Six
  95, 248, 357

Step Seven
  283, 309, 354, 357

Step Eight
  70, 94

Step Nine
  70, 80, 210, 212, 285

# INDEX

Step Ten
    107, 139, 181, 214, 256, 264, 284

Step Eleven
    20, 159, 160, 279, 306, 314, 316, 320, 325, 337, 341

Step Twelve
    97, 215, 238, 272, 275, 282, 342, 355

Strength
    18, 41, 135, 170, 242, 275

Stress
    244, 247, 256, 349

Support
    51, 274, 324, 326

Surrender
    19, 124, 187, 202, 220, 242

Tools
    35, 40, 69, 113, 328

Traditions
    73, 175, 274, 275

# INDEX

Trust
    13, 33, 62, 112, 114, 117, 119, 121, 169, 170, 174, 192, 207, 216, 222, 223, 234, 319, 320, 347
Truth
    42, 66, 283, 313, 328, 340, 360
Turning it over
    13, 39, 145, 169, 191, 198, 208, 237, 239, 241, 307
Twelve Steps and Twelve Traditions of Alcoholics Anonymous
    369
Twelve Steps of Co-Dependents Anonymous
    18, 54, 56, 84, 93, 112, 163, 172, 215, 275, 367
Twelve Traditions of Co-Dependents Anonymous
    368

# U

Unmanageability
    51, 65, 152, 165
Unworthy
    73, 108

# INDEX

Values
    204, 299, 330
Vulnerability
    33, 112, 180

## W

Willingness
    29, 45, 70, 93, 94, 122, 159, 187, 277, 279, 308, 339
Wisdom
    24, 25, 41, 59, 66, 114, 122, 149, 202, 215, 259, 312
Worry
    29, 39, 107, 228, 241, 252, 276, 295